BREAKING THROUGH

BREAKING THROUGH

FINDING PASSION AND PURPOSE
AS AN ASIAN AMERICAN

CHRIS GUO

NEW DEGREE PRESS

BREAKING THROUGH

Finding Passion and Purpose as an Asian American

ISBN   978-1-64137-126-1   *Paperback*

            978-1-64137-127-8   *Ebook*

For my parents. Thank you for your unmeasurable love and support.

CONTENTS

INTRODUCTION

———

"Growing up, some of my mom's friends would tell her that she was wasting everyone's time by letting me play so much basketball," Jeremy Lin said. "And so she would get criticized, but she let me play because she saw that basketball made me happy."[1]

Little did Lin's mother know, her little boy would grow up to become the star of one of the most memorable periods of professional basketball in history, called "Linsanity." It also sparked a nationwide stir, especially among young Asian Americans.

As of 2015, 20.4 million Americans identify as Asian Americans. In fact, the U.S. Asian population grew 72% between 2000 and 2015, the fastest growth rate of any major racial or ethnic group (for context, the second-fastest-growing group — Hispanics — grew 60% during the same 15-year period).[2] Curiously, this growth seems to have gone largely under the radar.

"Asian American" is a pretty broad term, though, given that 19 different origin groups or countries make up 94% of the 20.4 million. The largest group is Chinese, making up 24% of Asian Americans, or a shade under 5 million. Indian Americans make up 4 million or 20% of the Asian population, while Filipinos account for 3.9 million or 19%. Asian Americans originating from Vietnam, Korea, and Japan each represent more than 1 million Americans. Evidently, Asian Americans consist of a diverse group of people who share both cultural similarities and differences.

In early 2012, Jeremy Lin went from no-name benchwarmer to instant NBA sensation. Promoted to the starting line-up, thanks to a mix of trades, injuries, and luck, Lin was given the opportunity of a lifetime. And oh, did he shine. In his 12 starts before the All-Star break, Lin would average 22.5 points and 8.7 assists. He propelled his New York Knicks to a 9-3 record during those games as well as earning the team a playoff spot.

For me — and these 20.4 million other Asian Americans — Jeremy Lin's magical run of games was a moment of unique excitement, hope, and potential. Why? Because Jeremy Lin, like me, was born and raised in the United States to Asian immigrants: his parents from Taiwan and mine from China. Lin was the first Asian American to make it big in the NBA. Having shared a similar background to him, I felt empowered and inspired that Asian Americans could find success in the most untraditional of ways. Since I had grown up with so few Asian American role models in almost all areas of popular culture, it was a breath of fresh air to finally find one in one of my favorite sports.

I consider myself *both* American and Chinese. You might call me a Chinese American or, more generally, Asian American. In contrast, my parents would identify less with America because they had spent all their lives in China until they moved to the United States for graduate school. For them, it was much harder to fit in when they moved here, and they have continued to retain many of the traditions and cultures of their home country. Meanwhile, I grew up watching Spongebob and playing football. It seems many of my experiences growing up fit the picture of a more traditional "American" childhood.

There were many moments, however, when I felt trapped between the two worlds of China and the United States. Some of this had to do with being perceived as "foreign." I always worried that my parents would hold up the line at the cash register because the cashier couldn't understand what they were saying. Other aspects stemmed from subtler cultural differences in my parents' approach to parenthood. For example, asking permission to sleepover at a friend's house usually was rejected with a firm: "No. Why don't you go play piano or do workbooks instead?"

I also had split friend groups. The suburb I grew up in near Cleveland, Ohio, was decently diverse, with a 78% white, 10% Asian, and 10% black ethnic breakdown, so I had my crew of white friends and then separately my group of Asian friends. As I grew older I became more conscious that the two groups would rarely mix. My Asian American friends were like me, sons and daughters of Asian immigrants to the United States. The story I usually heard from them was that their parents came to this country either for graduate school or right afterward to find work. They settled down in Cleveland because they found jobs here. Because of the pre-eminent Cleveland Clinic hospital system, a lot of my friends' parents were doctors. And there were also many whose parents were scientists like my father or engineers. Growing up in this kind of environment, I was not explicitly told but still deeply indoctrinated with the idea that becoming a doctor was one of the only ways to achieve stability and economic prosperity.

"It's funny because once I got into Harvard, the same moms that were criticizing [my mom] were asking her questions about which sports their kids could play to go to Harvard. It was a funny reversal for me to see them support me in basketball, even though not many other Asian parents would have done the same," said Lin.

For these moms, sports weren't an activity for fun, health, and character building, but instead a way to improve their kids' chances of getting to a prestigious college. The parents would never want their kids to try to play the sports professionally. That was much too risky. Rather, medicine and engineering were held up on a pedestal as the ultimate goals. Sports and extracurricular activities were merely means to other ends.

Lin's parents had a different mindset when he first started playing basketball. He began playing because his father, who had a fascination with the NBA, would take Lin to the local YMCA to shoot hoops. His father instilled in him a love of the game, while his mother was more involved with his playing when he was older. She was the one to tell coaches that Lin would not practice unless he received good grades, *and* she helped start an elite-level youth basketball program for her son to compete against the best players.[3]

Perhaps Lin got lucky to have such supportive parents, but his path from high school to Harvard and then NBA stardom wasn't as smooth as it seems, either. Lin was good enough in high school to receive scholarships from top basketball schools. But, as he described, "I'm not saying top-5 state automatically gets you offers, but I do think [my ethnicity] did affect the way coaches recruited me. I think if I were a different race, I would've been treated differently." At his first SF Pro-Am game, where scouts look for talent and even NBA players play for off-season practice, someone told Jeremy, "Sorry, sir, there's no volleyball here tonight. It's basketball."

So Lin never ended up receiving any Division I scholarships. Harvard eventually recruited him but gave no scholarship. He proved the college scouts wrong and made the most of his time at Harvard by making the All-Ivy League First Team his senior year and becoming a finalist for the Bob Cousy Award for the most prolific point guard in college basketball.

Again, he fell short when he wasn't drafted to the NBA. Instead, Lin played in the NBA's developmental league and worked his way up, eventually signing a deal to play for the Golden State Warriors in 2010. He received little playing time and again bounced between the D-League and NBA. Finally, he ended up on the New York Knicks at the end of 2011. The culmination of all this work was in February 2012 when he shocked the world with Linsanity.

His path to the NBA was in no way easy, and that's what makes his underdog story so appealing to me and a generation of young Asian Americans. Not only did he achieve success through a non-traditional route, but he also overcame racial profiling through grit and hard-work. Although he hasn't replicated that Linsanity performance since, Lin has firmly established himself in the rotations of the NBA teams he plays for; he currently plays for the Atlanta Hawks on a three-year, $36 million contract.

In 2015, 61% of Asian Americans in the labor force over the age of 25 had bachelor's degrees. The second-highest number was 39% for whites, a whopping 22% difference.[4]

Again there is a stark contrast in statistics between Asian Americans and other ethnicities when it comes to occupational categories. 51% of Asian Americans work in management and professional careers compared to 40% for whites. The numbers are 30% for blacks and 22% Latinos. Furthermore, the median annual household income of households headed by Asian Americans is $73,060, compared to the U.S. average $53,600.[2]

Asians are also more likely to pursue entrepreneurship than other major racial/ethnic groups, but less likely than whites to be self-employed. In 2015, 9.6% of Asians were self-employed compared to 8.3% for Latinos and 5.2% for blacks. The number for whites was 10.9%. The rates of self-employment for Asians declined from 11.0% in 2000. Perhaps this change is due to a decrease in low-skill service businesses like restaurants, beauty salons and grocery stores; instead, there is an increase in high-skilled, professional-type businesses. The percentage of Asian Americans who were self-employed at incorporated businesses was 4.0%, the same number for whites.[5]

From the data, we see that Asian Americans as a whole are better educated, have higher incomes and work in more solid professions compared to other ethnicities: We've figured out some formula for success.

Or so it seems.

First, any numbers involving Asian Americans as collective group must be taken with a grain of salt. We might see trends among Asian Americans overall, but these trends may not hold true for certain sub-groups. This discrepancy is especially apparent when comparing median household incomes. For example, Burmese Americans have a median income of $36,000; in contrast, Indian Americans have almost triple that amount with a median income of $100,000.

Because in general Asians seem to be doing well, these numbers have led to the perpetuation of the "model minority" stereotype. You may have heard these stereotypes about Asians before:

- Asians are smart. They excel at math and science.
- Asians work hard and become doctors, lawyers, and engineers (and in 2018 they become investment bankers and consultants).

- Asians are quiet and nerdy. They aren't fit for management roles. They are more of the heads-down worker type.

These stereotypes apply pressure for Asian Americans to go into the stable yet prestigious careers mentioned above. If you don't, then you are labelled a "dumb" or "not good" Asian.

Furthermore, the glowing statistics for Asian Americans mask the fact that on average Asian Americans are less likely than other ethnic groups to be promoted to management. A 2018 Harvard Business Review article explored the data behind Asian Americans and management roles. In fact, they found that Asian Americans are least likely to be promoted to upper management. "As one example, Goldman Sachs reported that 27% of its U.S. professional workforce was Asian American, but only 11% of its U.S. executives and senior managers, and none of its executive officers, were."[6] And it>s not just the finance industry, but law[7], technology[8] and other industries as well. Another study found that "although they were 6 percent of the population and 6.5 percent of the labor force in 2011, Asians held only 2.4 percent of the total board seats in Fortune 500 companies; only 18 Asian Pacific Americans held CEO positions."[9]

The "bamboo ceiling" is a term coined by author Jane Hyun that refers to the "combination of individual, cultural, and organizational factors that impede Asian Americans' career progress inside organizations."[10] Adia Harvey Wingfield, a professor of sociology at Washington University in St. Louis, calls it a "racialized sort of glass ceiling."[11] It seems that Asians are labelled prematurely as unfit for management and thus not considered for such roles. In essence, Asians can get into great roles at first but find it tough to move up.

Before Jeremy Lin, I didn't have many Asian American role models as a kid. Other than my dad, my main source of Asian role models was popular YouTubers KevJumba, Nigahiga, and Wong Fu Productions. Sure, there were Asian actors like Jackie Chan, but they played overly stereotypical roles. There were also very few popular Asian music artists or other famous figures. Growing up as a kid who listened to his dad say, "Investment bankers make a lot of money" and then parroted that career goal on his college admissions essays, I never really questioned what was possible. After all, it's hard to aspire to other fields if there is a lack of representation and role models. Until Jeremy Lin became an overnight sensation and suddenly made me — and millions of other young Asian Americans — question what I thought I knew. Lin showed me that anyone could shatter and break through the bamboo ceiling.

And it led me on a quest — a quest detailed in this book — to offer a look at other Asian Americans who have broken the mold, done something different, and pursued a path that "made them happy." Along the way I've been able to hear stories such as:

- Ken Kamada's desire to play Division I football at Boston College instead of attending Harvard.
- Suzee Han's decision to drop-out of medical school and go straight into venture capital.
- Chloe Kim's path toward Olympic Gold, while making her parents as well as millions of both South Korean and U.S. fans proud.
- Ray Fung's self-proclamation that he is the "Bruce Lee of hairstyling."
- Kaitlyn Yang's Blockbuster card, originally intended for her to learn English, that led her to become the co-founder of a Hollywood visual effects studio.

Over the past year, I've been fortunate enough to interview, research, and study over 100 of the most unique, successful, and creative Asian Americans today. And while it might be easy to say their paths were all different or unique or the products of good fortune, something else exciting emerged.

A pattern.

Inside this book, I'll share the surprising commonalities of these unique and successful Asian Americans — and the lessons you can learn to apply to your own journey. My hope is that you can find a pathway that fits your interests, your experiences and your goals to become the next Jeremy Lin,

Chloe Kim, or John Cho.

Join me on this journey to meet some of the most incredible, unique, and awesome Asian Americans I could find — people just like Jeremy Lin — who have broken the mold and offer all of us a roadmap to follow to break our own bamboo ceilings, to do something a little crazy, and to find our own way to happiness.

My hope is that any of you reading this book will realize you might go on to be the next Jeremy Lin and pave the way for generations of Asian Americans to come.

Let's find your path together.

HOW TO USE THIS BOOK

———

This book is designed to offer you a framework for finding your passion and purpose in life. Use this book as a tool. That means you can jump around the chapters and read the parts most fitting to you. If you read the whole book from front to back, however, you'll get a fuller picture of Asian American struggles and triumphs.

My hope is you will find two things:

A path (or multiple) that you most identify with, that you can "fit" yourself to, learn from, and follow.

Whatever you believe is the purpose of life, it doesn't hurt to be happy! As you will see in many of the stories to come, happiness wasn't achieved until people took risks and pursued what *they* thought would make themselves happy and *not* what others and the world expected of them. Growing up, when I asked people what I should do in life they responded, "Find what you are passionate about." That response never sat well with me and seemed too cliché. The question in my mind was always, "*How* do you find and pursue what you are passionate about?" The answers I received were never satisfactory. Instead I sought out the answers and was able to narrow down five paths to success for Asian Americans discussed in Part I:

The Good Kids

These are Asian Americans who have grown up learning there is a set path to life. Often the end goal is to have a stable, well-paying, and prestigious career. As kids, they follow this path because it seems to make sense and it's what they know. However, later they realize their desires deviate from "the path" and internal conflict ensues.

The Rebels

Because the world and their parents say, "You can't be this or that," they actively try to defy stereotypes. Often, the Rebels reject or even hate being Asian and instead strive to become more like the white majority. In the process, they realize their motivations are flawed.

The Trailblazers

These people have a strong desire to pursue what they love, often defying stereotypes to do so — except they face discrimination in their fields from others, regardless of merit. Asians lack representation in many areas of popular culture and the Trailblazers want to change that fact.

The Ignored

As we learned, the model minority stereotypes make certain Asian sub-groups invisible. This phenomenon is a problem because these people are expected to be something they are not and they many not receive the support they need. In addition, people who feel pressured to be a "certain type of Asian," even when they aren't, fall under this category.

The New Majority

While the Trailblazers have paved new paths for Asian Americans having dealt with discrimination in their fields, the New Majority are Asians who are comfortable in and feel accepted by their communities. Having adapted well to mainstream society, these Asians might even seem be the norm. However, they sometimes feel lost among the cultures they belong to.

As you discover your path, you might realize you belong to

more than one, so don't feel pressured to be defined by only one path.

A set of role models to look to for guidance and support.

In Part II, I examine the stories of successful Asian Americans from each path. Having Asian American role models is important because we often grew up without them. Thus it was hard for many of us to find people with similar upbringings who went on to do crazy awesome things.

A study on role models in 2008 explains that "our sense of what is possible in our careers is influenced by what has gone before, how we interpret that history, and how we draw inspiration and learning from leaders past and present in our own identity development." In addition, "for minority populations, it can be difficult to find leaders perceived as sufficiently similar or desirable to emulate, and hence those individuals will lose out on the potential benefits of having a role model."[1] As you can see, having role models is imperative, and the earlier we find them, the better.

WHY DID I WRITE THIS BOOK?

My goal is to inspire young Asian Americans to achieve success in life by finding what they are truly passionate about. I am a college student myself, so I can't say I've achieved the highest success yet in my life. But what I can do is interview and research successful Asian Americans and distill their thoughts and experiences into revealing narratives on the Asian American experience. In other words, I wrote a book that I would have wanted to read as a high school student or freshman in college.

The next question you might ask is: "Why write a book on success through an Asian American lens?"

You might already partially know the answer, but I believe identity and upbringing play a large role in how people find and pursue their passions in life. For Asian Americans in particular there are certain stereotypes perpetuated by the media and society and ourselves. One example of such a stereotype is that Asian parents pressure their children to become doctors, lawyers, or engineers. I can't say that every Asian American has dealt with the same societal and parental pressures as I have, but many Asian Americans have at some point found a conflict between what parents preach, what stereotypes shout, and what being both Asian and American means.

Another goal for my book is to undercut misconceptions and stereotypes about Asians and, by doing so, demonstrate to Asian American youth that stereotypes should not and do not define them.

So, to summarize: I am writing a book on finding passion and purpose in life as an Asian American because Asian Americans often face similar struggles in their identity, which lends itself toward a different and unique journey in finding success and happiness.

WHAT IS AND ISN'T THIS BOOK?

There are plenty of books that attempt to help you become successful through a step-by-step guide. That is not this book.

This book is an account of interviews I held with successful Asian Americans in a variety of different fields, traditional and non-traditional, and a compilation of research outside of interviews. My goal was to find a broad array of Asian Americans because the Asian American experience is vast. It goes without saying, but not everything in this book will directly apply to you. Still, there are undoubtedly themes and messages that you will find applicable. Ultimately, you will get out of this book what you choose to get out of it. This book will make you question the way you think about life and purpose. It will change your mindset and that will leave a more lasting impact on you.

HOW DO I DEFINE SUCCESS?

In high school, success to me was getting a 4.0 GPA, setting school records in swimming, doing summer volunteer work or part-time jobs, having friends, and finding a girlfriend. In college, success for me was getting a 4.0 GPA, finding a prestigious internship and eventually job, having friends, and finding a girlfriend.

When talking about success the conversation eventually leads to the topic of careers, which makes sense because jobs are how most people make a living and define their accomplishments. In this book I measure success by how much achievement someone has made in a career that they are passionate about and that fulfills his or her values for life.

With this definition, success is unique to each individual. You can define success how you want. At the end of the day, if you truly believe you are successful, then you are. That's why I can't give a cookie-cutter, step-by-step guide to how to achieve success. I was looking for such a formula when I was younger, but I've realized since that such a mindset is naive. We are all shaped by our varying experiences and thoughts from the moment we are born, so in this book I let each individual story's message shine through themselves.

PART I: FIND YOUR PATH

CHAPTER 1

THE GOOD KIDS

———

Susan Ho's childhood was split between the United States and China. In the beginning, her family immigrated to the United States so her parents could attend college at Arizona State University. To pay for tuition, Susan's father worked part-time as a busboy and her mother as a waitress while they took classes. She recalls that they only had $20 maximum for weekly groceries. Sacrifice, it seemed, was necessary to achieve the "American Dream." After living in America from age 3 to 12, her family moved back to China, and later she attended boarding school in Boston.

When Susan was younger, she had a plethora of different interests. She wanted to become a painter, an entertainment lawyer, and a pop star. But her parents taught her from a young age that there was very much a set path to life. There are jobs that are acceptable and others that are not. Their only dream for Susan was for her to get good grades, find a stable 9-5 job, and start a family.

Susan's dream of becoming a pop star was in fact not too far off. While she was living in China, she was able to get a producer and even landed a record deal. But, in her words, "you have your Chinese parents who are kinda like, 'Yeah, no, you're gonna study for your SATs; you're not gonna call that producer back.'" When Susan told me this I was shocked, even slightly angry. Why would her parents say that? How could they just crush her dreams so quickly?

However, Susan explained to me that her parents' words and support were more important than something she saw ultimately as a hobby. Her parents were the ones who drove her to and paid for singing lessons, so if they didn't support her pop singing career, then so be it. Put simply — she understood the plan her parents laid out for her life and accepted it: get straight A's, find a stable career, start a family.

As a good, obedient child, Susan listened to her parents and never ended up signing the deal.

I call Asian Americans who listen and comply with what their parents' dreams are for them the "Good Kids." They don't actively try to run away from the expectations placed on them by the world and instead accept what people have told them their entire lives. However, they end up feeling lost when they grow older and must decide what they truly want to do in life.

They typically have immigrant parents who are strict and authoritative, parents who demand perfection, especially in academics. In turn, the kids listen to and internalize what their parents say. They are also usually high achievers: valedictorian, president of the speech and debate club, captain of the tennis team. Despite success in many different areas like sports and music, however, they usually end up becoming doctors, lawyers, engineers, or having any other prestigious, traditional career.

Perhaps your parents told you to pursue a certain career and you obliged because you hadn't previously thought about what you wanted to do in life. But now, you are starting to have doubts. You've lived your life pretty well until now. You've done well for yourself, but you feel unfulfilled. Can you imagine going into a field that you would be apathetic toward or hate because your parents forced you into it? At the same time, how do you confront your parents about your desires that directly contradict theirs? Big or small, there's a conflict in our minds: continue to do what my parents want me to do and hope it eventually works out or go out and pursue what I want for myself and my own happiness.

Susan set out to achieve what her parents wanted for her, and so she attended Wharton School of Business at the University of Pennsylvania. After college, she worked at Boston Consulting Group (BCG), one of the top consulting firms in the world. Even though she didn't get to see her dream of becoming a pop star come to fruition, she was still very successful on paper.

Of course, there were bumps along the way.

Her first internship in college was at an investment bank in Beijing, which she ended up hating. Instead, she worked in a fashion industry internship the summer after her junior year. Susan had been interested in fashion growing up and even ran a club at Wharton dedicated toward fashion, bringing in moguls from the industry to speak to students. The junior-year internship is usually considered the most important because it often sets people up for a full-time career in that internship's field, so Susan was taking a risk in going down a less traditional route. Her parents were not on board. They refused to give her much money for rent and food during the summer to show her how the pay would be if she did fashion full time.

From the outside, a job in fashion seemed glittering to her. But, after three months at her internship, she figured out how to do her coworkers' jobs in half the time. She realized she didn't want to do fashion full time (at least not right out of college) because it was not challenging her. In addition, once she was on the inside of the fashion industry, she realized it wasn't as cool as it seemed. She wanted to be surrounded by the best of the best people and those people weren't in fashion.

When you are young, learn as much as you can and surround yourself with the best people.

After, as she says, "squandering her junior-year summer internship," Susan realized she needed a job change and pursued consulting full time instead at BCG. She was back on the path her parents approved of — but it was her own decision. Susan wanted to do something where she could learn useful skills that could be applied anywhere and where she could be surrounded by the brightest people. She said that BCG was the perfect place for that, calling working there "the best decision in terms of [my] career." Her advice to college students is to come into a job with a mindset of humbleness. She says, "When you come out of school, you don't know anything." It's less pivotal what role you have in your early career and more important that you find a job that will teach you a lot and equip you with applicable skills.

I can relate to Susan's story because my father had his own plan for my life and he told me about it multiple times growing up. I was a pretty decent swimmer in high school and my father's goal for me was to do well in both swimming and school, so I would seem unique and well-rounded to the colleges I was applying to. It was my choice whether I was to swim in college or not, but for him swimming was a means to get into the good colleges. Like Susan's parents who rejected her singing career, my father told me, "You will never be a professional swimmer." It sounds harsh, but I knew what he meant. It's incredibly difficult to be number one in a sport and I'm not genetically gifted like Michael Phelps. Furthermore, there's very little money in professional swimming. Yes, it would be super cool to be a professional athlete, but I listened to my dad because he was being practical and I understood his rationale.

In high school my dad attended every one of my swim meets and recorded all my races on video. We would watch the swims later that night and analyze my stroke technique. I would try to implement his stroke improvement suggestions for me in practice the next day. My dad also wrote down goals for me to reach at the end of the season. Sometimes it was overbearing, but I also knew it was good for me. I appreciated the amount of effort my dad put into helping me succeed.

My mom also contributed her part as well. After practice, there would always be a home-cooked meal. Most days she would prepare three to four different traditional Chinese dishes with a healthy blend of meat, vegetables, and carbs. She would wash my swimsuits, goggles, and towels every night by hand, and always made sure to ask if I was feeling okay. Sometimes she would even tell me to stop training so hard because she could tell I was exhausted! For this care, I was grateful. I knew my friends' parents did not have the same level of commitment as my parents did.

In response to my parents' expectations I ended up breaking three school records and placing in multiple events at the state championship meet. If I were to examine my motivation for swimming, much of it came from my desire to fulfill the expectations that my parents had for me. Their expectations were, of course, also high for activities outside the pool as well. They demanded perfect grades in school, and I worked hard to achieve that as well.

It wasn't all sunshine and roses, either. Although I understood my parents' expectations, there were many times when I would argue that the way my dad wanted me to swim in practice was different from what my coach wanted. "Dad, how can you tell me the coach is wrong when he's been coaching for 20 years?" was a frequent personal retort of mine.

Another time, in my freshman year of high school, I got a C on an English essay. When my parents saw the grade, they first yelled at me to work harder and to look at "all the other kids" in school who were doing better than me. They then declared that they would call my teacher to set up a conference asking why I wasn't excelling. I had to beg them for hours not to. I didn't want them to take it upon themselves to deal with my own bad grade. I did, however, take this C as a great learning experience.

Learn to get over bad grades.

This advice is hard. Very hard. Especially because when I got bad grades I would never hear the end of it from my parents. A bad test for me would kill my mood instantly for the day. My heart would pound looking at the test score and soon my mind would be flooded with doubts of my intelligence and how I would have to explain it to my parents. Yet I've learned that you just have to go to sleep and start the next day afresh. There's nothing you can do to change the grade, so move on. Understand that if your parents yell at you about grades it's because they care. Although it always sucks to be chastised, you should understand your parents are trying to help you out for the future.

But, wait. Isn't this book all about the paths the crazy, unique, and oddball Asian Americans take to success in different careers and professions?

Yes. You see, it's important first that Good Kids understand that their parents only wish the best for them. Understanding your parents means having a better relationship with them built on more trust.

Parents are not the enemy.

This can be hard to keep in perspective, especially when their goals deviate from your own. Instead, change your mindset to: "I want to work hard and not only make my parents proud of what I've accomplished but also be proud of myself." The enthusiasm with which you do what you love will shine through to your parents.

Parents aren't unreasonable at all in their goals for their children. They want to see their children lead lives of decent and stable comfort. Jennifer Lee, professor of sociology at Columbia University, explains why parents, especially immigrants, hold these beliefs: "They do so because they come from countries where education is one of the *only* paths for mobility. And, as non-white immigrants in the United States, Asian immigrant parents fear that their children will experience discrimination in their careers. So parents shepherd their children into conservative, high-status professions in which they may be most shielded from potential discrimination by employers, customers, and clients."[1]

In the end, you have the final decision on what you want to do in life whether your parents support it or not — but your parents aren't purposefully trying to make you feel bad or overly pressure you.

And sometimes our parents are right. If being a doctor, engineer, or lawyer turns out to be your calling, then good for you. With a lot of people, though, there is a point at which they either realize they aren't cut out for the job or they aren't passionate about it. Susan complied with her parents' goals for a long time, but eventually she started taking some risks (to her parent's dismay, at first) toward pursuing something better for herself.

Susan quit working at BCG after two years to join the startup Fab. When she first joined Fab, her mom cried because her only dream was for Susan to continue on that stable path.

When Susan was a kid living in the United States, she recalled seeing her mom study for her MBA (in English, which was her second language) until 1 a.m. and then wake up at 7 a.m. to bring Susan to school. Since her dad was working all the time she didn't see him much either. "My parents struggled, so I could have an easier life," Susan explained. Because she saw their struggles, she did feel like she should listen and conform to what her parents wanted for her life. Yet Susan's mindset started to change as she grew older: Her parents didn't want her to stick to a certain path just for her to be unhappy. Instead, they wanted her to follow that path because they thought the security and comfort would make her happy.

In the end, however, her parents would be even more glad to see their daughter do what she really wanted to do in life as long as she was truly enjoying it. **Susan claims it would be a waste of her parents' hard work if she didn't get to whole-heartedly pursue what she wanted.**

Susan came to this realization because of her understanding of and empathy for her parents. As you can see, it's okay to take a couple risks; eventually, your parents will come around to it.

So, start small, but take bigger and bigger risks.

Susan's story shows us that Good Kids can succeed and overcome conflicts they have with their parents about their career if they first prove themselves capable of success, whether that's on the path they want or the path their parents want. If you never show to your parents that you can achieve, they'll continue to pressure you to go down the traditional road.

In any situation, you can't be mediocre, especially if you go down a different route from your parents' expectations. Your parents will start telling you to become a doctor again, and you'll get mad, not just at them, but also at yourself. Why? Because you agree with your parents to a certain extent. You want success and a career that pays the bills, just like they want you to have. You just want that career to be something that you love as well. Very rarely will you be happy in a career that your parents never come around to because you share their belief that you should be successful — that's how you lived your life for so long before you started to become a little rebellious.

If you do want to change paths, eventually you need to take some risks to find what you love. But the risks don't have to be crazy. A lot of people dream of quitting jobs, switching career paths, and just starting all over again; this route might not always be the best idea. Instead, if those risks are calculated and thought through, then they could prove life-changing.

Susan did exactly that when she decided to leave Fab and start her own company: Journy, an online travel concierge service. Her idea for Journy came from other passions of hers: travel and food. While it was a big risk to start a company, she had already proved to her parents and more importantly to herself that she could succeed.

In the beginning, however, it was tough. Her startup wasn't taking off, so her parents of course told her to quit and get a normal job. Because they saw her working so hard with nothing to show for, her dad bluntly told her, "You are dumb." But Susan understands that "[these comments] come from a place of love. It's just their way to show it."

With Susan's faith in herself, Journy eventually started gaining traction, and she soon landed a spot on the Forbes 30 under 30 list. Her parents' gripes over her career choice were starting to slowly wane.

So how did Susan find so much success?

In her words, "Really hard-work. I will brute force my way through anything." She pulled all-nighters at BCG. Her first week at Fab she did two all-nighters. Her mindset was to never give up.

At one point when Susan was running Journy, the company was facing a shortage of money. One of her investors invited her to a party he was throwing in LA, so she took a flight there. When she arrived, she realized she had $50 left in her bank account and nowhere to stay. "What am I doing with my life? My startup is failing, and I have no money. What am I going to do?" Susan wondered.

Susan believes that most people would have given up at that point, shut down the business, and found a stable job. Susan decided, however, that she was going to fight until the end, and, in fact, things began to look up from there: The hotel Journy partnered with ended up letting her stay the night for free. That same night, she met Dave McClure, the founder of 500 Startups, at the party. Within their first conversation, McClure said he was going to invest $200,000 in her company.

Her company was back on its feet. Was there luck involved? Yes, a little. Yet even so, she wouldn't have gotten to that point without hard work in the first place.

As Lebron James says, "Nothing is given; everything is earned." Unfortunately, sometimes there's no magic formula, and it takes some grit and hard work to succeed. But that doesn't mean wasting your time on things that are unimportant. Some people are just not born or wired like Susan, with the ability to work incredibly hard and pull all-nighters. I've learned that anyone can work hard, however, by making their time efficient.

Here's a couple hacks:

Multitask on things that can be multitasked.

Listen to podcasts while cleaning your room. You are supplementing a mundane task with an educational one.

Stop bringing your phone around.

If you are working, don't bring your phone to work. It's both a distraction and a time-eater. If you are a student, don't bring your phone to the library. If possible, don't bring your computer either. If you need to read a book, then just bring the book! If you need to read an article or notes on your computer, print them out and leave the computer at home!

Schedule things for the morning.

This tip applies to night owls like me who find it hard to wake up early. If you schedule important meetings or appointments in the morning, it will force you to get up and start the day earlier. Be warned, though, if you are a student, this advice might not work with early morning classes!

Remember and write down your motivation.

It's easy to get caught up in the moment and forget why you work or why you study. Whether your motivation is to provide for your family, work toward a better future for yourself, or just because you like what you do, remind yourself why you work instead of complaining about being tired.

Susan Ho is an example of someone who was a "Good Kid" for a long time. She got into a good college and got good grades. She started getting a little bit more independent when she pursued her junior-year internship in fashion. But it only seemed like an attractive job from the outside. Eventually, she decided to listen again to her parents and join a prestigious company like BCG, not just because her parents wanted her to, but because she wanted to learn a lot, gain skills, and surround herself with other high-achieving people. While consulting wasn't her ultimate passion, it did prepare her for future endeavors and was a good experience for her career.

Eventually she did find a job she was passionate about that would also pay the bills, which was starting a company involving her love of food and travel. Her parents weren't completely supportive at the time, but listening to them for a long time growing up and proving that she was capable of success helped her parents be less worried about her.

CHAPTER 2

THE REBELS

———

"Hey Chris, what do you want to be when you grow up?"

"Something in business. Maybe investment banking," I responded every time apathetically.

Up until junior year of college, I dreaded this question because I was lying each time I answered. I did not want to be a banker because that job didn't excite me at all. But this disinterest didn't stop me from being singularly set on it as a career as early as sophomore year of high school. Why?

First, I had a strong desire to be different.

In high school when I was thinking about my future career, I immediately crossed off certain options in my mind. My older sister wanted to be a doctor, as did many of my friends in high school. However, in my mind, I didn't want to be seen or characterized as a stereotypical nerdy pre-med Asian kid. So first I rejected medicine as a career path. As you can see, I didn't reject medicine because I wasn't interested in it, but just because I didn't want to do what everybody else was doing. Not a good idea.

Similarly, I didn't want to become an engineer because I thought that was too nerdy for me. Keep in mind, I was and still am a huge nerd. I'm proud of the long hours I put into playing Runescape and Pokémon. Okay, maybe not so proud, but again, at that time I wanted to be different from all the other Asian kids. Perhaps part of it was feeling ashamed of my ethnic identity and wanting to be accepted by the white majority. Within stereotypical high school hierarchy, nerdy types aren't exactly at the top of the social pyramid. Added into the mix was a race dynamic that was already beginning to emerge at that young age, where Asians also aren't at the top. I wasn't as acutely aware back then, but I did know I wanted to be cool. That translated into acting more like my white friends who weren't in my mind "nerdy," so I arrogantly rejected the Asian stereotype.

I desired to be different because I was hyper-focused on how others perceived me. So even though I didn't want to become a doctor, I still wanted to pursue a prestigious job — just not one that everyone else was doing.

Ironically, it was my parents who introduced me to banking. My dad mentioned to me that bankers make a lot of money and he thought that I would be good at the work they do. None of my other friends ever mentioned wanting to work in finance, and it wasn't the classic doctor-lawyer-engineer career path I had heard about so much as a kid, so my mind was made up. Something about doing the same thing as everyone else wasn't good enough for me.

In my mind, I have been a mold-breaker from a young age. I was the only Asian kid on the tackle football team in fifth grade. In junior high, I was one of a handful Asian boys singing in choir. There was a point when I was singing in three different school ensembles and playing alto saxophone in jazz band and taking weekly piano lessons and studying for Science Olympiad and training for swimming.

That didn't mean I was slacking in the school department either. I was the top student and I got a lot of pleasure knowing that I was not only successful but also stereotype-defying because of my other activities. Thus I felt that my accomplishments and decisions made me "better" in some way than the other Asian kids who better fit the Asian stereotype of "nerdy." My deviation from the normal stereotype, I thought, would make me more impressive in the eyes of others.

Important to note: I wanted to be perceived as cool and therefore buck stereotypes because *society arbitrarily devalued the typical Asian stereotype as uncool.* We can't help but develop these stereotypes, especially if we grew up in the U.S. Evidently, I had flawed motivations for being different. I was basing my actions on how people perceived me instead of what I wanted to actually do. But, it would've been difficult for me at the time to see the extent of how stereotyping had already affected my thoughts and actions.

Because of my addiction to how people viewed me, banking seemed the perfect fit. It was unique in my mind and made a lot of money. When I was a freshman at Northwestern University, I was focused completely on school work and how the extracurricular activities I did would boost my resume. The end goal, of course, was to get a banking internship and eventually a full-time job in finance.

Even more ironically, I soon realized I was not as different or stand-out as I thought because a lot of people, including Asians, wanted to be investment bankers. It was becoming more apparent to me that my motivation for wanting to become a banker was totally wrong.

My freshman year I also joined an entrepreneurship club called EPIC in which I participated in a year-long accelerator program whose goal was for students to launch a business within a year. I was only vaguely interested in entrepreneurship at the time, but I was hungry for anything to put on my resume.

The business I started with three other freshmen was called Party in a Box, a e-commerce party supply company. The start-up ultimately failed, but I garnered a new appreciation for the entrepreneur life, something I had no knowledge of before. I was learning new terms and concepts like "business model canvas," "iteration," and "failing fast." When we first came up with the idea for Party in a Box, I remember being unable to sleep. I was too busy thinking about ideas for the business. What was the business model going to be? What would the website look like? How were we going to get inventory? It was exhilarating and so much more rewarding than the classes I was taking — and, of course, investment banking.

Entrepreneurship really hyped up the part of me that always wants to be different and mold-breaking. In turn, my investment banking interest waned more and more.

During the program, the leaders showed us an advertisement that gave me shivers. The ad is from Apple's Think Different campaign in 1997. Here's the transcript of the ad for reference:

Here's to the crazy ones.
The misfits.
The rebels.

The troublemakers.
The round pegs in the square holes.
The ones who see things differently.
They're not fond of rules.
And they have no respect for the status quo.
You can quote them, disagree with them,
glorify or vilify them.
About the only thing you can't do is ignore them.
Because they change things.
They push the human race forward.
While some may see them as the crazy ones,
we see genius.
Because the people who are crazy enough to think
they can change the world are the ones who do.

Nowhere in the ad does it talk about Apple or Apple products. Instead it highlights the people who are different or who think differently. The people mentioned in the ads are those whom I call "Rebels." These people end up becoming business leaders, entrepreneurs, creators, and innovators because they refuse to be normal and enjoy being different.

Asian American Rebels sometimes see both the negative and positive stereotypes associated with Asian Americans as something to beat and thus desire to be different from others, especially other Asians who act more stereotypically. Often this wish leads them to excel at not only at stereotypically

"Asian" things but also non-stereotypical activities like football or singing.

Because Rebels understand that stereotypes can be harmful, their response is to run away from them. The problem with this thinking is that the process of actively defying Asian stereotypes causes them to forgo or even hate their Asian culture. Their motivation becomes twisted; they try to act "whiter" instead of being true to themselves.

What I've noticed, however, about the most successful Rebels is that they don't focus on their Asian-ness much. Their motivation isn't about being different because they are Asian. Instead, they talk about their humanness and the hacks they have used to make themselves into successful people. They thirst to be successful by taking a different path.

There were three main lessons I learned from talking to these successful Rebels:

First, to thrive as a Rebel, don't let defying Asian stereotypes be a motivation. Focus instead of improving yourself as a human.

I saw this firsthand when I rejected certain career paths because I thought they were too "stereotypically Asian." Instead of exploring what I potentially could've been interested in, I ran away without trying. My value was very much rooted in how people perceived me and thus I didn't get to find what I truly loved to do. Instead, if you want to be a difference maker, desire to do so because you want to improve yourself as a human and because you want to help other humans. Serial entrepreneur Ken Kamada states it best: "I identify first with being a human being."

Second, Rebels have ideas and want to make a difference. If you have project ideas then go out and DO IT.

Growing up the Midwest, I hadn't heard much about students starting companies in high school or college. Or, when I heard about college dropouts like Mark Zuckerberg or Bill Gates, I wrote those people off as geniuses. They achieved success that I couldn't possibly achieve. I was content with chugging along through my classes and just doing well on the only path I had known for my entire life: get good grades to get a stable, well-paying job.

When I got to college and saw firsthand students just like me start businesses while also taking classes, I saw a new side to my future. There were so many more paths available to me, like being my own boss and not having to sit at a cubicle all day. It was liberating. I often thought how my life would be different if only I had been exposed these ideas earlier.

The summer after my sophomore year in college I wanted to

pursue my own passion project in conjunction with trying to be an investment banker. I was going home back to Cleveland that summer and by that time I was getting more and more interested in entrepreneurship. So interested, in fact, that I also had a goal to film a documentary on startups in Cleveland. That sounds crazy coming from someone who had no experience filming anything except five-second clips to send to friends on Snapchat. It was also crazy for me because I knew that to make a documentary I would have to do a ton of research and networking.

It's funny because "networking" is a big buzzword in the banking world. If you talk to someone who has gone through investment banking recruitment they will most likely mention the word "networking," most likely with a disgusted look on their face. Basically, students will email any banker they can get in contact with, asking for a 30-minute phone call or coffee chat to "ask questions" about what the job is like. The truth is most students aren't curious about what the bankers do. They just want to make a connection with the banker in hopes that he or she will recommend them to the recruiting office.

For me, networking was terrifying. I did not want to cold-email a 40-something-year-old managing director at a bank who lived in a mansion and probably didn't give a damn about what a freshman in college was curious about. So, up until my sophomore year summer I didn't. Some of my friends were already doing over 50 coffee chats with bankers, and I was feeling behind.

Promising myself that I would not make my summer a waste of time, I mustered the courage to fire off emails to some bankers. For my documentary I looked up startup founders in Cleveland and emailed them. Most of the bankers ignored me and my conversations with the ones who responded were boring. But when I talked to a founder of an artificial intelligence startup I found myself intrigued and genuinely interested in the conversation. I could talk to him without being overly professional, and I could also ask questions different from the cookie-cutter ones I was asking the bankers. I ended up doing way more chats with people in the entrepreneurship world than in banking.

Summer went by fast and I ended up not filming the documentary because I soon realized it was too big a project for that short a time period. But, I took all I learned about Cleveland's startup scene and wrote a blog on Medium about it. It gave me a sense of pride that I was able to produce quality content about something I was passionate about after putting in the time to do the research.

By refusing to have an unproductive summer and going out of my way to start a project not assigned to me by someone else, I further explored my interest in entrepreneurship — which aligned much better with what I was truly interested in.

Finally, whether you fit in more at a more traditional job or not, what matters is focusing on what you value.

Reflect on your motives for your goals and pursuits. Part of my motivation to become an investment banker was because of my desire to not fall into the Asian stereotype of being a doctor, lawyer, or engineer. In my head I wrote off other career paths before fully considering them. If you are doing the things you do just to not fall into an Asian stereotype, then stop. By striving specifically to prevent a stereotype from defining us, we paradoxically allow the stereotypes to have greater power over our actions. Be independent and make the decision yourself to do what you truly want to do without the influence of others. What will make you fulfilled and happy?

Don't let a desire to either buck or fulfill external expectations change who you are as a person, though. Remember that you are a human being first. You have goals and desires that shouldn't be affected by this. Instead of actively running away from being Asian, embrace it. For some, ethnicity is a bigger part of their identity than others. But for anyone, it's important to embrace at least a little of that aspect of you. Be proud of the food you grew up eating, who your parents are, and your childhood experiences.

You have strengths as a Rebel, so take advantage of them. You like to be different, which means you are good fitting in anywhere, more adept at navigating social situations, skilled at thinking creatively and differently. Take this advice and pursue roles that align with your values.

CHAPTER 3

THE TRAILBLAZERS

Fact: Asian American actors and actresses are underrepresented on TV and in film, and even if Asian Americans are portrayed in the mainstream media, they are often not given the starting role.

Opinion: We need more representation in media! There are of course exceptions: John Cho, for example, defied stereotypes in 2014 by becoming one of the few Asian American males to play a romantic lead on TV in the show "Selfie." But these people are few and far between.

The "Trailblazers" are those who push the envelope and challenge stereotypes by succeeding in non-traditional roles despite encountering discrimination that prevents them from moving forward.

In media, Asian women are "exotic" and fetishized, while men are discounted for being unattractive in the white Hollywood sense. In business, there's the "bamboo ceiling," the phenomenon in which stereotypes of Asians as quiet and not fit for leading cause many to see stagnation in their careers.

John definitely faced racism throughout his acting career. He said in a Reddit AMA post in 2014, "I experienced racism, and in my professional life, I try to take roles (and have always tried to take roles) that don't fall within the parameters of any Asian stereotype...And so to me, hopefully, that's a positive thing I can put into popular culture and so maybe in some bizarrely tiny way that helps people not think of Asians in one particular way."[1]

As one of the few successful Korean American actors in the US, he saw firsthand the discrimination in the industry. A 2017 team of researchers studied 242 TV shows and 2,052 series regulars in the US. They found that Asians are usually missing, have low visibility, and are tokenized. 64% of shows researched didn't feature an AAPI (Asian American Pacific Islander) series regular. In contrast, 96% of shows had at least one white series regular. The study also found that "87% of AAPI series regulars are on-screen for less than half an episode." In addition, "68% of TV shows featuring AAPI series regulars have ONLY 1."[2]

Similar findings are seen in film. According to a USC report, "Of the top 100 films of 2015, 49 included no Asian or Asian American characters" and none of the leading roles were played by Asians. Only 2.8% of films studied had Asian directors compared to the almost 6% Asian population in the United States.[3]

The discrimination is perhaps most blatant when white actors play Asian characters. Emma Stone's portrayal of Allison Ng in "Aloha" and Mickey Rooney as Mr. Yunioshi in "Breakfast at Tiffany's" have even been termed "yellow face": white-washing of roles meant for Asians in film and TV.[4] However, John was not only able to add Asian representation to TV by acting as a lead but also break through stereotypes as a "romantic" as opposed to comedic (or kung fu master) lead.

Born in Seoul, South Korea, to Korean parents, he moved to the United States with his family when he was young. John grew up in LA and attended UC Berkley, graduating with an English degree. Out of college he moved back to LA and started small roles in films (fun fact: John popularized the term "MILF" in his role as "MILF Guy #2" in the 1999 film "American Pie"). He later gained more popularity starring as "Harold Lee" in the comedy "Harold & Kumar Go to White Castle."

But later he realized something about his roles. "For a while, I was feeling like I was always playing characters that weren't specifically Korean or specifically Asian even — that they were characters who were originally written white and then they would cast me. And I used to consider that a badge of honor because that meant I had avoided stereotypes. And then on the other hand, as I got older, I started to become resentful that they weren't written Asian. And so their family history doesn't quite match up. It exists in this, like, cinema fiction that their name is Smith but they're — has an Asian face and their character history doesn't seem authentic. And it all felt — I was having a problem feeling like, this doesn't feel real."[5]

John was noticing a less blatant but still prevalent form of racism within Hollywood. Asian Americans actors and actresses often have to play white roles because there is a lack of roles written specifically for Asians. Apparently, it's easier to sell and market a movie that people are used to with white leads and roles.

There's no perfect solution to the issue, but after researching many of the successful Asian Americans who overcome racism in their work I found some common ways they have navigated the discrimination.

Speak up.

Like John, the most successful Trailblazers are truly the best at what they do since they love it so much and often push back against racism. They speak up because they feel a need to help those in similar situations.

We all have to do a better job of raising our voices. It's easy to just view discrimination as a fact of life, a permanent presence in society way too big for any single person to change it. Yet actionable change needs to start with spreading awareness and fighting for justice. Many of the most famous Asians in media like John talk about racism in the industry to push back against discrimination.

Don't perpetuate stereotypes if they don't fit you.

Go against the grain. But don't do so solely to be a social justice warrior. Go against the grain because discrimination prevents you from moving forward. If you love acting, singing, or anything else and a racist industry prevents you from success, continue to do what you do because you love it. Your intentions should not be solely to break racial stereotypes. Instead, keep working hard at what you do because you believe in yourself that you are meant to succeed.

Find mentors or role models.

This advice is harder as an Asian American because often when we think about role models, we think about famous people in media and entertainment, exactly where Asians are underrepresented.

On the positive side, you can see the representation growing with shows like "Fresh Off the Boat" and movies like "Crazy Rich Asians," in which there are more Asian actors and actresses. But there is still so much more room to grow from here.

Perhaps there would be more Asian American representation in media, but because potential actors and actresses were told by their parents from a young age that these roles weren't fit for them, those people never got to pursue their dream. They never had role models on TV or in media to begin with and aspire to become, so they just submitted to their parents' desires.

Cho also stars in the 2017 indie movie "Columbus." The Korean American protagonist Jin played by Cho arrives in Columbus, Indiana, a quaint Midwestern town famous for its interesting architecture, to see his father on his death bed. He befriends a girl one year out from high school who is struggling with her own issues.

For Cho, the perfect depiction of Asian Americans doesn't completely ignore them, nor does it feel overburdened as a commentary on race. Instead, the presence of the Asian Americans should seem natural, as if they're meant to be there.

This representation is tough to achieve, however. Cho notes, "I've found this with some Asian American writers: They want to defy stereotypes, so they write in opposition to it, but the stereotype is still a strong chain, even if it's less visible...It's hard in America as a writer of color, an actor of color, not to get caught up in race and culture. But you're also supposed to be able to write characters and scenes in a way where it's just a matter of fact, a component."[6]

Yet "Columbus" had the perfect balance of not ignoring race while not focusing completely on it — the type of portrayal we should hope to see more of in Hollywood and in real life.

The role was perfect for Cho: "It's universal, and also super specific for me, the idea of the distant father. I've thought for years, sometimes against my will, about what kind of son I'm supposed to be, what's expected. Being Korean, that's a particularly charged question. Is your duty to your culture or to your parent? Is your life your own, or the second half of your parents' life? Who owns your life? Maybe the answers are obvious to some people, but not to me, and not to Jin. I didn't even have to try to think about relating; it was right there.

CHAPTER 4

THE IGNORED

___

The phrase "Asian American" was created in 1968 by UC Berkeley students during the Vietnam war. Its goal was to unite all Asian ethnicities on campus. At that time people would identify themselves by their individual countries. You would hear "I'm Chinese" or "I'm Japanese" or "I'm Filipino" instead of "I'm Asian." It made sense that people identified only with their own country, because unlike in the melting pot that is America, there was rarely any diversity of ethnicity in their home countries. The Berkeley students grouped all Asians into one identity because it "signaled a shared and interconnected history of immigration, labor exploitation, and racism, as well as a common political agenda."[1] It was easier to push for social justice and establish the voice of all Asian ethnicities in the United States as one larger group.

It should be clear that labelling all Asian groups under the umbrella "Asian American" didn't lead to Asian stereotypes in the first place. Rather, stereotypes had already formed in people's minds before the label and those stereotypes had already grouped all Asians together, ignoring ethnic difference. Whether formed because supposedly "all Asians look alike," ignorance to cultural difference, or because of Orientalism — Western exoticism and fetishism of East Asia — stereotypes needed to be addressed and it was easier to do so by mobilizing a larger group of voices.

You see, there is a chicken-and-the-egg situation here. The Asian American label was self-chosen by a group of students to rally together people similarly discriminated. Indeed, especially in recent years, certain Asian stereotypes have come to light and been addressed because of a push by Asian Americans for equal treatment. However, the grouping also contributes to the perpetuation of the stereotypes of the group as whole when the individual ethnic groups stand quite diverse in culture and lifestyle at times.

The "Ignored" are Asian Americans who don't fit the Asian stereotype. Whether that's in socio-economic status or not being "good at math," these Asian Americans feel they are looked over or expected to be something they are not.

Alex Wagner, author and co-host of *The Circus* on Showtime, explains, "This, more than shame, more than lack of resourcing, more than widely held stereotypes, may have more to do with Asian invisibility than anything else. Asians don't necessarily think of themselves as "Asian," and so the struggles of one subset of that group may not be particularly relevant at all — if they're even on the radar. Collective marginalization on its own can be a unifying force, but it assumes identification in a collective to begin with. And that's not necessarily the case as it concerns Koreans thinking about Bhutanese, or Indians thinking about Filipinos."[2]

It's important for the Ignored to remember not to forget about their American identity.

We are not just Asian, but Asian American. There is a part of us that values freedom and the "American Dream" because we are American ourselves. We also have a civic duty to vote and stand up for ourselves. Unlike our parents, we can be less concerned about the differences between racial subgroups and put more value in being a collective group because we are unified by our American experiences.

However, the "Model Minority" stereotype makes certain groups invisible in a perverse way. Sarath Suong is a Cambodian refugee and executive director of Providence Youth Student Movement. "Growing up during the 1980s and 1990s, the Asians we saw were East Asian, and often images of the model minority," he said. "And that never felt like us. We were failing out of schools, we were being harassed and profiled by the police, and there was a really fast school-to-prison pipeline — and now, a school-to-deportation pipeline...When I wanted to join Asian American groups, I always felt like I was othered by my skin color, my class, or my refugee experience...I've always felt, personally and as a community, rejected by Asian America."[1]

According to the NYC Center for Economic Opportunity, around 27% of Asian Americans in NYC live in poverty.[4] The national average for all U.S. citizens is 13% and 10% for Asians.[5] What the model minority stereotypes does is highlight successful immigrant stories and ignore a large population of Asians that don›t meet stereotype standards. Thus, while a lot of people need aid or federal support they are instead ignored since the "common understanding" is that Asians are doing just fine for themselves.

Furthermore, among all major racial groups, wealth disparity is highest among Asians. According to Pew Research, "Asians near the top of their income distribution (the 90th percentile) had incomes 10.7 times greater than the incomes of Asians near the bottom of their income distribution (the 10th percentile)."[6] Because of the model minority stereotype, this disparity often goes unnoticed.

In addition, the model minority stereotype puts a lot of pressure on Asians to succeed, especially in school. This burden can be particularly harmful if their strengths are more suited to a creative as opposed to intellectual field. Unfortunately, Asians have a disadvantage when applying to schools. A Princeton University study of 124,000 applications to elite universities in 2004 found that the "Asian disadvantage is comparable to a loss of 50 SAT points."[7] There's an expectation that Asians are supposed to be "smart," so the achievements of Asians are under-appreciated. With such high expectations, students also are less willing to seek help.

So how do the Ignored succeed in America?

First, we need to remember that we still have it better than our parents and we should speak up.

Our parents sacrificed for us. Remembering this fact makes you humble and more motivated to work hard. Believe that you can make yourself and family better if that's important to you. Being able to live in the United States is a blessing, and we have all the opportunity in the world to find and pursue what we want. Pessimists will say that America has faltered in recent years and is no longer a place where you can achieve the "American Dream," perhaps not only due to racial stereotypes but also less mobility by the system as whole. I don't agree — there is plenty of opportunity. Living in America, our mindsets can change and it can cause us to ignore the fact that the rest of the world does not have the freedom of mobility that America provides. We should be grateful for this freedom.

Furthermore, the Asian American population is the fastest-growing racial group in the United States. But we haven't been participating in our civic duty. "In 2012, only 47% of Asian Americans voted in the presidential election — compared to 66% of black voters, 64% of non-Hispanic white voters, and 48% of Hispanic voters."[8] We need to speak up as a racial group since we have the opportunity to. Speak up because you identify not just with Asia but with America.

Stop blaming.

It's often tempting to write off the success of other people. They got lucky. Their dad gave them money. They didn't have to grow up thinking about not having food to eat. In fact, we often hate others in success despite not knowing their full story. We conclude without evidence that these people haven't encountered failure before or they were wired to be successful.

So, we blame. Blame our friends, families, the system. We may even blame ourselves, but we still feel treated unfairly. The problem with blaming is you internalize this pessimistic attitude. If you blame being Asian for your failure or way you live it's only further perpetuating what you are lacking. If you blame racism for not being able to move up in your job, you gave up pushing on. So, stop the blame: Believe in yourself and your own merits.

There's no easy solution to the model minority issue. Raising our voices will help. That means all Asians should speak up (not just those negatively affected), just like those original UC Berkeley students envisioned 50 years ago.

CHAPTER 5

THE NEW MAJORITY

———

Chloe's face stung; her legs shook. It was too cold, and she felt out of it. But she couldn't quit now: There was too much on the line.

After falling during her final practice run minutes before the snowboarding half-pipe championship at the X Games in 2015, she *had* to focus. She shuddered as she replayed the terrible feeling of smashing her face into the ice like frozen concrete. On her first run, she fell again. Good thing she didn't hit her face this time.

But she didn't quit. She kept going. On her third run she notched the highest score of the competition. Chloe Kim, at the age of 14, became the youngest X Games half-pipe gold medalist.[1] Just three years later, at age 17, she would win gold in the half-pipe at the 2018 Olympics in Pyeongchang, South Korea.[2]

At the 2018 Winter Olympics, many Asian Americans burst onto the scene with stories that captured the hearts of many. We saw Chloe Kim win gold that year with grace, style, and swagger. The ShibSibs charmed us on the ice to earn bronze in pairs skating, and Nathan Chen dazzled with six quadruple-axel jumps in one program — a first at the Olympics for anyone. You know what I think? It's about time that Asian Americans became recognized for their amazing achievements beyond being seen as "nerds."

And it's not just sports where Asian Americans are making a name for themselves. As part of the fastest growing population group in America, we have started to make our mark in television, music, and business.

Ricky Yean, co-founder and CEO of Upbeat, tells it best[3]:

Fortunately over the last decade, I believe we're witnessing the beginning of the rise of Asian America. Every time Jeremy Lin attacks the rim and rocks a new hairstyle, he inflicts major damage on the stereotype. On Fresh Off the Boat, Constance Wu and Randall Park are showing off the eccentric Asian American family and making it something endearing that we can all be proud of. Eddie Huang and David Chang are the irreverent chefs with untouchable swagger. Ali Wong, Aziz Ansari, Kumail Nan-jiani, Ken Jeong, Mindy Kaling are the funny Asian Americans that you wished you were friends with. Steve Yeun, John Cho and Harry Shum Jr. are sexy men ready to be your next male romantic lead (#StarringJohnCho). We even have an Asian American running for president in Andrew Yang(!)

The "New Majority" are Asian Americans who feel accepted in their communities because of their experiences growing up and living in America. Over time, as more Asians find representation in all fields of pop culture and work, they might even become the norm. Cultural stereotypes are acknowledged, but don't necessarily define the New Majority. Instead, they have created their own unique culture that is profoundly both Asian and American.

Interestingly, demographics might have something to do with the rise of the New Majority. Across the entire US population in 2017, 5.8% of people identified as Asian (not including mixed-raced Asians).[4] However, in some areas, Asian Americans are the majority. For example, California "has almost *forty* places with more than 10,000 households and an Asian household percentage of at least 25 percent."[5] In certain suburbs within areas like the San Gabriel Valley and Silicon Valley, Asians account for over 50% of the population. California schools also have large populations of Asians. "At UCSD, for instance, 50% of undergrads are Asian. At UCLA and UC

Berkeley the percentage of Asian undergrads are respectively 40% and 42%."[6]

As a New Majority, Asian Americans are shedding the label of "minority" not just in in terms of population numbers, but also in terms of mindset. Up to this point, I've focused on how deviations from the stereotypical Asian American path has led to success and fulfillment. I have also discussed how Asians lack representation and often face discrimination. However, this is not to say that being Asian American is always an impediment. We don't always have to diverge from what's expected of us to find success, and we don't have to reject our own identity to find acceptance. There is a lot to be proud of as an Asian American, and that is the type of attitude that can lift a group of people from minor to major.

With the growing numbers of Asian Americans and increasing acceptance, the question becomes: what exactly *is* our culture? Part of the confusion has to do with a lack of culture to start with. It's tough to define Asian American culture. Do we have our own music and fashion, or do we just copy from other racial groups? This question is also complicated by the pervasive stereotypes that exists about Asians. How are we supposed to develop a culture for ourselves as Asian Americans without perpetuating stereotypes? How do we make Asians cool when we are viewed as nerds? Should we even try to make ourselves "cool" if that's not "who we are" or are we just victims of stereotypes again?

Yean has an explanation. Asian Americans, according to him, are "cultural orphans." Remember, Asian Americans weren't established as one group until the late '60s. Even then, it was just a label. Compared to other racial groups, we haven't had time to develop a culture of our own. Yean claims, "We don't know what it means to be Asian American, and so far we haven't shown much interest in figuring it out. On top of that, our parents would remind us that Chinese and Koreans detest the Japanese. Indian and Pakistani people don't get along. Generally the light-skinned Asians look down on the "jungle Asians" of South East Asia. Historically, we're just not that interested in being lumped into the same group. However, the younger generation of Asian Americans like me do not have this historical baggage. We're simply interested in finding our identity, but when we look out to the world, all we can find is the lazy portrayal of the uni-dimensional, kung-fu fighting, smart, obedient, emasculated man or hyper-sexualized woman. The Model Minority. That sucks."[3]

No culture is monolithic or stagnant in nature, and no doubt the identity of the New Majority will continue to evolve. But perhaps the answer is to embrace the parts of the culture that are ours now and that we have inherited from our ethnic heritage.

Embrace your Asian Identity

We are blessed to be able to share the Asian cultural roots of our ancestors, while also being able to have our own personal and uniquely American experiences. Because our experience is unique and diverse, it's important to be proud of both cultures we grew up in. Although these two sides can at times butt heads, a better understanding and appreciation can lead to increased acceptance of our roots and ultimately of ourselves.

One of the most admirable aspects of Asian culture is the collectivist attitude and devotion of families to the wellbeing of their children. The dark side of this is the often unrealistic expectations that parents set for their kids. Chloe Kim's story is a prime example of this. Chloe Kim is a second-generation Korean Americans born to two immigrant parents from South Korea. Hailing from Torrance, CA, she is also like any other teenage girl from LA, taking to Twitter to talk about how she ate two "bomb" churros to calm her nerves before snowboarding competitions. When she was eight, her father quit his job to help her become a pro-snowboarder. Her father sacrificed so much to help her become who she is, and Chloe was able to deliver under the greatest pressure. She successfully fulfilled the expectations of her father, herself, and the entire country of South Korea (imagine that pressure).

While this all sounds like the perfect fairytale, if you examine the story deeper, it's complicated. Her father literally had a plan for her entire life since she was a young girl. What if she didn't even like snowboarding when she was younger? Doesn't it also seem like he imposed his will upon her life? He also took a huge risk and made such large sacrifices on behalf of his daughter. What if she didn't end up becoming the snowboarder she is today? Would quitting his job be for nothing? That kind of parental devotion is touching in its own right.

Even though I'm not an Olympic gold medalist, Chloe Kim's story is relatable to me. Her father had a vision for her to become the best snowboarder in the world, just like our parents have ideas for our lives. I'm sure Chloe had her fair share of arguments with her father about snowboarding. She also must have seen that her father was trying to push her to reach her maximum potential, and there's no doubt that she is grateful for his support.

In a lot of Asian American success stories, we don't just see an individual effort, but also a team effort with parents and children working together to succeed. We aren't our parents, but we have much to owe them. There is something ineffable about the love Chloe's father has for her. It shines most prominently through his actions of waking up and driving five hours a day to take her snowboarding when she was younger. "Tiger Mom" parenting styles also come with the incredible devotion of our parents to our success and their unshakable belief that we are capable of achieving greatness. And that's special.

Sometimes we are reluctant to embrace our Asian identities because it has been tied to certain negative stereotypes. But having an appreciation for your culture does not mean stereotypes have to define or apply to you. In fact, it might be the opposite. You'll see differences between Asian and American culture and love both for what they are if you embrace your culture. Stereotypes will eventually just fade to noise in the background.

As a member of the New Majority, embrace your Asian identity and you'll find a greater appreciation for yourself, your parents and the world.

The immigrant mentality is an asset.

Part of the Asian stereotype stems from the fact that often people from Asian families are immigrants themselves or children of immigrants. Because the immigrant story is often one of hard-work in order to survive in a completely new environment, immigrants usually embodied the archetype of diligent, heads-down workers. So, don't think that Asian Americans are the only people who have strict parents who force them to work hard – there are plenty of others with similar situations because they are also immigrants or have immigrant parents. Hard-work is a necessity to achieve prosperity after starting from nothing.

It's great to have this immigrant mentality. You have a chip on your shoulder and a motivation to prove yourself through hard work. Again, especially if you feel as though you have been discriminated against as an Asian, nothing will be spoon fed to you. Hard work is still important to succeed.

Other Challenges faced by the New Majority

In areas where the Asian population is growing such as California, the culture and view of stereotypes is much different in these areas because no longer are Asians viewed as different, but instead the norm. But sometimes these areas are seen as "Asian Bubbles," where Asians primarily interact with each other. It's possible that living among a large population of Asians only further perpetuate stereotypes because of group mentality and limited exposure to others. The downside of bubbles is that they lead to a lot of competition, especially in school. Often Asians have doubts of their enoughness when so much value is placed on grades. They continue to stress and try to achieve academically because all the people around them are doing so.

Keep in mind that the idea of a bubble is not unique to Asian Americans. Everyone self-segregates to a certain extent and thus chooses who they do and don't see. Often the reason stereotypes are perpetuated is not that Asians don't want to interact with other cultures, but the reverse: Non-Asians don't make an effort to get to know Asian Americans.[7]

What's the solution? Diversify your experiences.

The fact of the matter is, everywhere else Asians are the minority still. Although its often comfortable to stay in the social circles we are drawn to, meeting and hanging around new people with different mindsets will help you grow. That involves making diverse friends — people of different race, gender, upbringings, and experiences. You'll learn more about yourself and other people this way. Learn to live outside the bubble because you might have to leave that comfort some-time later.

I want to be clear, the point of exploring outside an Asian bubble is *not necessarily to be more like the white majority, so that you are able to fit in better. But because you will better appreciate different cultures, which will help you appreciate yourself more and give you confidence in your own ethnicity.*

Another solution? Find role models.

We didn't see many Asian American role models as kids, which contributes to our lack of firm cultural identity. Other

Americans didn't see famous Asian Americans in media either except people like Jacky Chan, which led to perpetuation of those "lazy" stereotypes Yean mentioned. Because these role models weren't as prevalent in our earlier years, it becomes especially important to put in effort to find those Chloe Kims and Jeremy Lins to look up to.

PART II: ROLE MODELS

CHAPTER 6

MED SCHOOL TO SILICON VALLEY – THE GOOD KIDS

———

No path in life is the same, but finding role models who have successfully broken the mold in career and life is important. Role models show us what is possible and what we can strive to become. In this chapter, I highlight three students from Northwestern University who are all Good Kids. They all saw relative success throughout their early lives, but realized they desired something a little non-traditional, so they went out of their way to pursue it. Here are their stories.

Suzee Han was pre-med. She made the decision to become a doctor from an early age and since high school she had been singularly set on this goal. Most importantly, of course, her parents were thrilled their daughter wanted to be a doctor. She would have a stable, high-paying career. Perfect.

Suzee took Organic Chemistry, a notoriously tough course, in her freshman year of college and did well. Genuinely interested in science, she enjoyed the class and wanted to absorb as much knowledge as she could. By the end of her senior year she had maintained a high GPA, received a high score on the MCAT, and got into medical school. She was closer and closer to her goal of becoming a doctor. Her parents would be proud.

Surprisingly, Suzee is now a venture capital associate and never ended up going to medical school. She has co-authored a book and even taught a class at Northwestern as an adjunct professor only three years out of college. So, what happened?

Suzee's first two years of college were very much on the pre-med track. But during these years, she learned some photoshop and website coding as a hobby. At the beginning of her junior year, a friend saw that she had an eye for design and asked if she wanted to design a website for a new club at Northwestern called Project Pitch where undergrads pitch startups to get funding for their ideas. Suzee took the opportunity because she wanted the resume boost and because of her design interest.

Eventually, she got more involved in Project Pitch and ended up being the main person running it without much entrepreneurship experience herself to begin with. She thought it was odd that she was teaching people about entrepreneurship when the people she was teaching had the same amount of knowledge as her. Doing so gave her confidence, however. "For the first time I was beyond just being smart. I realized I was innovative and had passion for chasing dreams," she told me.

Suzee later became the president of EPIC, another entrepreneurship club at Northwestern. As president, she oversaw the first Northwestern hackathon WildHacks and two large pitch competitions. Because of her experiences in entrepreneurship clubs, she realized she had a "feeling of wanting to do more." And still, up until her last few months of senior year she was pretty much set on being a doctor. Suzee graduated a quarter early and started working at the Farley Center for Entrepreneurship at NU. During that time, she got a med school offer and she signed it.

At that time, her vision for the future was that she would become an MD and then build a healthcare startup. She still wanted to attend medical school, however, because she believed that there was no route in life except medicine for her. Understanding her strengths and weaknesses, Suzee knew she could study hard and do fine as a doctor but wouldn't fare as well as a lawyer or something else.

I asked her, "Was there are singular moment that swung you in the direction of entrepreneurship and venture capital?" She replied that there wasn't a concrete moment. But each project she did relating to entrepreneurship pushed her further from medical school because she realized there were more jobs and paths outside of a traditional medical route. She also learned throughout college that she could be good at things other than doing well on chemistry tests. Her increased sense of self-confidence gave her the mindset that she could go out and pursue other fields and be just as successful. If her goal was to spend another four years at school just to get a degree to start a healthcare company, wasn't that a huge waste of time? Instead she realized that if she wanted to, she could just start that company right after college.

A couple days later she made a decision to not go to medical school. Doing so many entrepreneurship-related projects helped her gain confidence in herself that she could do something different. Once she realized that she could start things, it was quick decision.

The harder part was telling her parents. For Suzee it was especially tough because she was an only child and she appreciated her parents so much for everything they provided. She didn't want to let them down. At first her parents were really mad, but after some tears the decision was final. In the end, her parents supported her decision because they just wanted her to be happy.

So, what can Good Kids learn from Suzee Han?

Confidence can be cultivated.

Suzee talks a lot about gaining confidence in her abilities. She realized she could lead and wasn't just a person who was just good at heads-down studying. Confidence isn't just an innate trait. It can be cultivated and grown. Often, Asian Americans are taught to keep their heads down and stay humble. I have noticed that for myself this has led to over shyness and a lack of confidence. The way to get better at something is to practice, which means doing things outside of your comfort zone. Tell a crush you like them. Dress crazy. Stop thinking about what others think about you. In effect, just say yes to all opportunities despite your doubts.

"Default to Yes."

If there are opportunities available to you, go a little outside your comfort zone and seize them. If Suzee had not said yes to her friend to make the website design for Project Pitch, she could have been in a completely different place in life.

So, did she regret being pre-med? Not at all. Her motto is: "Don't regret; learn from it." For her, being pre-med meant forcing herself to the extreme academically. Because she was doing well, she felt confident in her intelligence. She truly loves science and learning, so she never hated pre-med. But she didn't realize there was another side of her that loves innovation and leading until she actively explored those areas. Nobody can tell you exactly what to do, but exposing yourself to more experiences and subjects will increase the chance that you will find something new about yourself that you didn't know you loved.

Maybe it was lucky that Suzee had a friend who gave her this opportunity, but there are always such opportunities available. Suzee believes that if you don't actively take up the ones that come to you, you could be missing out on something that you didn't know you loved to do. Legendary ice hockey player Wayne Gretsky said it best: "You miss 100% of the shots you don't take."

* * *

Suzee had no regrets about what she did. But my friend Spencer Park wishes he had not been so rigid in his plans from the start. Spencer graduated in 2017 with a degree in material science engineering and trumpet performance. On campus, he conducted material science research and worked in R&D during the summer after his junior year in college. It seemed he was very much headed toward a profession in science.

Spencer's father immigrated to the United States with his family when he was 10, and his mother was born in Maryland. Spencer is third-generation Korean American and grew up in Davis, CA, a suburb of Sacramento.

Spencer considers his parents "traditional" and "conservative" in the way they raised him. Sometimes they would find creative ways to make Spencer study or read more: For example, because Spencer liked to watch TV and play video games, his parents invented "TV Money." Every time he read a book or played outside, he could earn "money" that he would use to buy TV time.

He also started getting into music at a young age — at first by his parents' demands. Spencer started playing piano at age five and his mother would sit next to him, watching him practice until third grade. (If you've ever had someone sit next to you while practicing, especially parents, you'd know it is incredibly irritating.) Later, Spencer picked up the trumpet and enjoyed it so much that he applied to colleges with great trumpet studios.

So, Spencer came into Northwestern as a dual-degree in trumpet performance and material science. At that time, he had a plan for the next 10 years of his life: He was thinking about pursuing a Ph.D. in Material Science because many others, including his parents, had completed higher education. After that he would go into a stable engineering job, get married, and start a family. Currently, Spencer is a consultant at data-driven consulting firm. So, what changed?

First, he had internships in material science and realized the field was boring for him. He couldn't see himself doing what he did at his internship for life.

Second, he wanted prestige. He saw his pre-professional friends in college going into prestigious internships, and he wanted that recognition. Although he was allured by the high life, he did more research on consulting and realized it aligned with what he was interested in: solving problems and thinking analytically. He had found something more interesting than the material science that was also prestigious.

I asked Spencer if has found what he wants to do in life. His answer is no. Although he is on a great career path, his goals now are to be better at relationships with other people. He also has short-term and medium-term goals to do music production and work abroad.

His advice: "Don't think too long-term. Don't lock in, otherwise you miss out."

Spencer also enjoyed material science classes like Suzee enjoyed her pre-med classes, but he soon realized that he didn't want to do research his whole life. Looking back, Spencer realized that maybe it was short-sighted to continue with trumpet and material science when he ultimately ended up in a completely different field. He wishes he were more open-minded earlier to pursue other interests. Having a plan for life is great and will give you a goal to reach, but sometimes it can make your thinking very rigid. It can prevent you from exploring things off the path that you might like better.

It's so easy to compare ourselves to others who have found success and make excuses for why we haven't reached their level of achievement. "They got lucky. They don't have to deal with the problems I have right now." Or we end up pointing out flaws in ourselves that prevent us from achieving that success. "I'm not a go-getter like them. I'm not smart. I'm lazy." We have these thoughts because we don't want to take the risks and make the effort necessary to achieve this level of success. We are too content with being comfortable. "What will people think of me if I change majors or quit my job?"

I'm here to tell you that anyone can become a mold-breaker and find success in ways they may have previously written off. It's not just the outgoing hustlers or the geniuses. It can be everyday people who are comfortable keeping their heads down and working hard. But when thinking about finding passion or purpose in life, they need to think about their values. What do you value in life? What is your why?

Let's look at someone who has been on the journey of finding his why.

* * *

Aaron Leon graduated from Northwestern University in 2017 with a B.S. in computer science. He has co-founded a nonprofit that helps female entrepreneurs raise funds, called Womentum, and is currently a software developer at an innovative tech company in Chicago.

Aaron was originally a chemical engineering major with a biotechnology minor and he planned to do pre-med. Aaron wanted to become a doctor because he knew he wanted to make a difference in the world. Specifically, he wanted to go into pharmaceuticals or pathological research.

At the suggestion of his high school friend Derek, he participated in Battlehack Chicago, a hackathon that hosts both students and working professionals. Aaron felt like he was tossed into the waters. He had been doing research on computer science education for elementary school children, but he had not done much programming outside the one programming class he took in high school. Luckily, he was matched with a good team, and although Aaron felt like he didn't contribute much, he placed second in the event. What he realized was that he was having fun at the hackathon, and he even decided to take the project home to dissect it and add new features. His goal for pre-med was to make an impact, but that would involve extra years of school and often research could be slow-moving. Because of the hackathon, he saw he was able to build something that could have immediate impact instead.

Starting sophomore year, Aaron switched his major to computer science. His same friend Derek was attending Babson College, a school focused on entrepreneurship. In the winter of Aaron's sophomore year, Derek came to him with the idea of Womentum. Derek wanted Aaron to build a prototype website. Again, Aaron felt that same feeling he had at the Hackathon where he had no idea what he was doing, but this time he wasn't under a time constraint. So, he spent the winter learning to program better and built the prototype website for Womentum.

I asked Aaron if he wants to be a programmer for life. His response was that he doesn't care as much as long as he is making some social impact. He wants to help change others' lives for the better. Aaron believes he would get the most value out of life perhaps through doing more work in nonprofits. He sees a lack of tech in non-profit and he believes he could make a difference in this sphere. He believes tech is awesome because it makes things accessible and can be used as a tool for good.

Another of his goals is to tear down certain social constructs that have bound this generation of young people, especially the construct of pre-professionalism and always striving toward more money. One extreme goal he has is making a ton of money and giving it all away. I quipped, "And buy a boat for yourself while you're at it?" But he responded, "No, just give it all away." He thinks it's sad to see people spending their whole life building up everything just based on money and so-called success.

As he was working on Womentum, he first felt, "Oh, I'm just a student doing this little side project. Anybody can do this if they tried." Aaron at first didn't feel the impact of his work. Later, however, one woman who got funded sent an update of her dressed in her graduation gown. That picture really impacted Aaron. Realizing if one person near Chicago nowhere near Africa could help someone get their diploma, Aaron believed he had potential to help a lot of people through tech.

So, has Aaron achieved success? In the traditional sense, yes. He has a nice full-time job and even started a nonprofit in college. Yet what's most important is his why. Perhaps he won't be a programmer for his whole life or maybe he will. But he knows for him, the most fulfilling experiences are those that help drive social impact.

Understand what your values are.

It doesn't matter what they are, but it matters that you know what they are; it's true. Some people do seriously only value money and an outward showing of success. It's not a bad mindset to have. But all too often, those values are the world's expectation of people and not what people truly desire and value.

Aaron values leading social impact. For others, it might be starting a family and being an amazing parent, or it might be always learning and challenging themselves in different ways. The definition of success is individual and stems from the values each person has developed throughout their experiences in life.

This fact is true for all humans, of course, not just Asian Americans. Perhaps Asian Americans might hear from the world that they should be "model minorities" and pursue prestigious traditional roles like medicine or law, but there are expectations and stereotypes placed upon every single human, and so what cuts through the BS is focusing on your value and where you truly get your worth.

This discovery might take some introspection. But knowing yourself first is vital for truly understanding your passions in life. "He who has a why to live for can bear almost any how," said Frederich Nietzsche. In plain English, if you have a reason or purpose for life, you can face any challenge life brings you.

* * *

Asian parents are famous for being strict and demanding. This generalization isn't true for every parent, but let's hear the perspective of one particularly strict parent: a "tiger mother." Amy Chua is a second-generation Chinese American parent, the author of *Battle Hymn of the Tiger Mother,* as well as a Yale Law School professor. According to Chua, children should just listen and comply with their parents who know what's best for them.[1]

This belief **isn't** what you want to hear. You want to hear about how to prove to your parents that you don›t have to pursue a traditional path in life. Amy Chua, however, quite directly says, "Chinese parents believe that they know what is best for their children and therefore override all of their children›s own desires and preferences," and "What Chinese parents understand is that nothing is fun until you›re good at it. To get good at anything you have to work, and children on their own never want to work, which is why it is crucial to override their preferences."

Chua is blunt, but I have to agree here that most classes, jobs, and activities are more enjoyable when you are good at them.

The hardest class I took in college was an econometrics class where I spent hours understanding regressions, omitted variable bias, and probability limits. I probably spent the most amount of time on this class compared to any other and when it was all said and done I ended up getting high marks in the class. Reflecting back, it was grueling yet fulfilling. Whereas I had thought I wasn't smart enough to do well in the class, through hard work I proved that I was just as good if not better than the people I always saw as smarter than me or naturally talented at school. Similarly, I used to practice over 20 hours a week for swimming in high school and being able to win a race back then was incredibly satisfying and something I will always miss and cherish.

Listening to your parents sucks when you want to be independent and make your own decisions, but Chua speaks some truth. Parents want their kids to be successful and have lucrative, stable careers. My dad always told me, "Money alone won't make you happy, but you're not going to be happy if you don't have any money." In other words, the best job would be one that pays well and makes me happy. But, a job that pays well and doesn't make me happy is better than a job that doesn't pay well because then I wouldn't be happy because of bad financial circumstances.

For Chua, "just because you love something...doesn't mean you'll ever be great. Not if you don't work. Most people stink at the things they love." As an adult, Chua has seen much more of the world than her kids and has learned that it's incredibly important to have a good work ethic — which means that as a mother, Chua made sure she instilled the discipline of hard work in her kids at whatever cost.

The moral of the story is your parents want to wish you the best. They want to see you succeed in some area that will provide financial comfort and hopefully then happiness. Once you have achieved success or proven that you have the capability to achieve success, then if there is something that you are really passionate about it's more likely that your parents will accept your pursuit of it.

Be grateful.

You'll have disagreements and fights, but eventually it's necessary to remember where your parents are coming from. If your parents are immigrants, they likely had to sacrifice a lot just to make it to the United States. Never be ungrateful for what you have been given. Just living in this country is amazing; we have the freedom to make our lives how we want to live them.

Sometimes your parents are right. When they are, acknowledge it. If they are wrong, then understand where they come from. When you are an adult you can live the life the way you want. You can even cut off connection with your parents. Just don't do so unless you know for sure you won't come crawling back. So, change your mindset and be patient and understanding of your parents. It's easy to be bitter toward tough parents, but imagine the hardship they went through to raise you. I'm not a parent, but I know it is not easy to raise a kid. As humans, sometimes parents are right and sometimes they are wrong.

I have a friend who in elementary school told me that his goal was to go to Harvard and become a doctor. Obviously, his parents had some influence in this goal. Still, he often told me that he watched videos online of surgeries and read up on diagnosing diseases. It seemed he had genuine interest in the field.

During winter break of our junior year in college we were playing ping-pong in my basement and I asked him, "Remember in fourth grade when you told me you wanted to be doctor?" His response was complicated. His father wanted him to be a doctor and nothing else. While he grew older he realized he didn't want to be forced into a job hand-picked by his parents. Instead he wanted to come to that decision himself. In an act of rebellion, he told his parents he didn't want to be doctor. They still were insistent that he take pre-med classes.

Later, my friend actually did realize he wanted to pursue

medicine, but he didn't want to tell his father that he was again pursuing that path because it would in effect be caving to his parents' set plan. He didn't want his parents to be in complete control of his life. So instead of acknowledging that what his parents chose for him happened to be the right path, he continued to not give his parents this acknowledgment. This mindset is the wrong one to have because it only causes resentment instead of understanding of where your parents came from.

I even told my friend that he should give his parents more credit, but he was adamant. Fortunately for my friend, he also found something that he loves even more. Every dollar that he made working jobs in college he spent toward skydiving. He loves it so much he now is a certified skydiving instructor, and he hasn't even graduated college yet. I'll cut him a little slack!

Again, there's no easy path to success. But starting on a path you love is the first step.

Even if you find what you want to do in life, there's no sub-stitute for hard work. Don't expect opportunities and luck to come your way. Instead, make opportunities and make luck: Don't just work hard, but work above and beyond what others do. That might mean working on side projects after work or classes. Maybe that means anticipating what your boss wants or always looking for ways to improve on processes at work.

If you've been doing things the same way for a long time and are getting bored, you can probably do something to improve the way you have been operating. Still, starting the journey toward your goals is magical and rewarding as long as you put in the work.

CHAPTER 7

HARVARD OR FOOTBALL? – THE REBELS

———

When Ken Kamada was a senior in high school in 1993, he was accepted to almost every Ivy League college. For most, this feat is unattainable, and the select few who do get into these top schools pounce on the opportunity to attend.

Ken, however, was different.

His dream was to play Division I football at a great football school, perhaps even a harder feat for him given his size. At 6 feet tall and 185 pounds, he felt underestimated. People around him said he was too small and wouldn't make it in college as a football player.

He would prove all the doubters wrong when he turned down going to Stanford or Harvard and instead enrolled at Boston College on a football scholarship. He became one of two Asian Americans at that time in 1994 to be playing Division I football. It was his dream come true.

His parents were shocked, however, and when I asked him how the talk with them went, his one-word answer was "terrible." For his parents, being able to say their son went to Stanford or Harvard gave them validation and hope that he could get the best education to eventually get a nice job down the line. His parents still hung on to their disapproval until his early 30s.

Ken Kamada is someone who totally breaks the Asian stereotype mold and perhaps at times purposefully made decisions in order to do so. But let's examine what his motivations were. Was he actively trying to break stereotypes, or did he just really want to play football? How much did being Asian affect his actions and decisions? Where did Ken's inner drive come from?

First, he didn't want to put a financial burden on his parents and thus wanted to take the scholarship to Boston College. Secondly and perhaps more pivotally, he had the mindset that he wanted to overcome all odds. He wanted to go against the grain and be better than what people expected of him.

Ken was born in Tokyo and bounced around between Japan and East Africa through second grade because of his father's work. Eventually, his family settled down in Bellevue, Washington, a suburb right outside Seattle, in the mid-1980s. When he first went to an American school he was placed in ESL despite being able to speak English well. His father was one of the first people to study English in Tokyo and his half-Portuguese, half-Chinese mother was from England and spoke perfect English. Ken felt overlooked because the school in the United States just assumed he wasn't able to speak English. Throughout his upbringing he felt pigeonholed because of his label as an immigrant. So, having felt discounted his whole life, he wanted to prove to others that he could overcome his differences and be successful.

I was curious if part of his motivation was centered around actively trying to break Asian stereotypes. When I asked Ken what he thought about being Asian American, he answered me this: "Our responsibility as a different race and class is to break down those barriers and identify with the fact that we are human first and have a heritage of being Asian. I think about that always, because if we want to break through those stereotypes, we have to identify as being human beings first." For Ken, stereotypes disappear when you view yourself as human-first. This mindset changes your motivation. No longer is your goal to break through Asian stereotypes because you perceive society places them on you. Instead, you choose what you truly want to be or do in life without thinking about stereotypes. If what you do or become breaks Asian stereotypes that's great. If not, that's also fine. As long as you have a human-first outlook, you'll be liberated from the effect of stereotypes on your decisions. That's not to say that you will no longer face discrimination because of your race, but your motivations no longer hinge on being Asian.

Perhaps Ken is different because he wasn't exposed to Asian stereotypes early on as a result of his background. He has a picture of himself from his school in Kenya and he sticks out like a sore thumb because he is the only non-black person in the photo. Because of his diverse upbringing, when he got to the United States he immediately connected with all shapes, colors, sizes. "I didn't see myself as Asian, but I thought of myself as someone who would become an American," Ken explained. He was labelled as an immigrant, yet he never thought of himself as one. While his parents disagreed with what the perfect Asian should be, they never discouraged him from being a human first and from being American.

Ken hasn't run away from his ethnic background either but instead acknowledges that it is part of who he is. He explained to me that his wife is white and from Detroit, yet two-thirds of the food they cook is Japanese. He believes his wife does not perceive him differently because he is Asian but rather sees him as her husband who happens to have a different cultural upbringing.

So how did Ken take this mindset and apply it to his life besides football?

In college, Ken was pre-med and a philosophy major. Philosophy was his own choice and pre-med was to appease his parents. His uncle was a cardiothoracic surgeon, so his family wanted him to become one as well. In college, he was top of his class and scored better than 99% of people on his MCAT. Just as with undergrad, he had success applying to medical school and was accepted to all the prominent schools. Meanwhile, he was playing football and running track. Because of summer training, he didn't have much professional experience like internships during college. During the summers, his goal was just to make some money. By his senior year, he felt burnt out — mentally and physically exhausted. He talked to his parents about taking a gap year as a break, an uncommon practice then. Ken didn't have a place to stay after college because his parent had recently divorced and his dad wanted to move back to Japan.

In April 1998, right before his graduation, he reset his post-college expectations. He wanted to go into the workforce for a bit to get some money, take a break, and then later transition to medicine. Just by chance, he got a job at Morgan Stanley after talking to some friends who were in the business school. He didn't know anything about investment banking and stocks, but Morgan Stanley gave him a chance. He believes he was hired because he told the interviewers, "If you put something in front of me, I will figure it out." His experience as a top student and serious athlete set him up to be successful.

Little did he know that investment banking jobs aren't exactly the jobs you take if you want a break. In fact, they are notorious for 100-hour work weeks at busy times. Nonetheless, he continued to work hard, following his mantra "Always be ready."

Ken had all the attributes necessary for success — amazing work ethic, great experiences, and internal motivation. But had he found his passion, had he found the life he wanted? For Ken, being American meant you could go after your dreams; you could work your way up and make your life the way you wanted. The life he wanted after a couple years in investment banking and deep introspection was to be his own boss and start his own company. Medical school was no longer in the picture for him either, because he already been out of school for some time.

If he took a leap of faith and started a company, he could work for a couple years and live modestly on the income he made from his work at Morgan Stanley. If he made zero sales at his startup, he would be broke at 31. Because he was a perfectionist, it bothered him to be 5-6 years behind his peers at 31. From a risk-reward perspective, the reward was being able to get control of his life; the risk was having his company fail, so he would have to find a new job. But that wasn't too bad a risk for him because he was confident his work ethic would be there to help him start over.

Ken chose starting his own company, a wealth management firm, which eventually became successful. Over the past 10 years he has been CFO of several software companies and has had 12 years at his wealth management firm. Currently, Ken is a venture partner at Harvey Partners, LLC, and he continues to run his business. He is living the life he wanted.

What can Rebels learn from Ken Kamada?

Be human first.

At the end of our talk, Ken made sure to emphasize again, "I identify first with being a human being." Because if we look at ourselves as human beings and live as good human beings, race and stereotypes become meaningless. You can identify as being Asian American but identifying as a human being allowed him to make the most of the opportunity to get the life he wanted.

What Ken is saying is that when viewing yourself as human first and setting aside race for a second, you look at the world differently. No longer are you thinking about Harvard and Princeton as being the "golden ticket." No longer are there expectations from the world that you must be a certain person. You can truly self-examine and think about what you want to do in life.

Do some self-reflection.

Take out a notebook and write down your dreams for five minutes. Not only for career, but for all aspects of life. It took a long, drawn-out couple of years before I realized for sure I did not want to be a banker. If you are doing something that you don't love, you really have to do some introspection. That self-reflection involves thinking about your values: Do you want to start a family someday? Do you want to travel the world? Do you care if you're making six figures or five? Do you want to startup a business? Forcing yourself to write down your goals will cause you to truly analyze what you want with your life.

You can be an entrepreneur, banker, doctor; it doesn't matter... but you need the confidence in yourself to believe you can do the work that you do and don't want to do something else just because other people are doing it or telling you to.

* * *

Hiro Kawashima's story is all about being faithful to his values, and we can learn a thing or two from his value-oriented mindset. His values led him to work at GE for five years on the commercial side and then eventually become the CEO of a startup called Prescience Health.

Hiro was born in Japan and grew up in Tokyo until the age of seven when his family moved to Chicago. As a child, his parents constantly told him that he needed to work hard to succeed in life. He took this advice to heart and it manifested as a hustler attitude. In seventh grade, he taught tennis lessons to 5-6 kids a day. He worked during the summers at Kumon — a tutoring company — and Nordstrom. He also started his own side tutoring business for kids during high school and developed an entrepreneurial attitude because he wanted to take the things that he was good at and profit off it by providing a service that others needed.

In high school, he started a project called Supplies for Dreams, a nonprofit that has donated over $200,000 since 2009 to the cause. He himself was attending a school where he was fortunate enough to have great access to resources; he noticed, however, that other schools in Chicago and particularly one in the South Side had students unable to afford school supplies. Noting this disparity, he decided to come up with a solution: His freshman year of college, he turned Supplies for Dreams into a nonprofit because he wanted his project to have a long-lasting impact. Today, Supplies for Dreams remains partnered with Chicago Public Schools to provide students with supplies they can't afford.

Hiro doesn't talk a lot about his Asian American identity, perhaps because he doesn't see it as a barrier to his success. It's a common theme among "rebels": They don't use their Asian American identity as a crutch for not achieving success. And it's not that they believe they achieve in spite of their race. They believe in themselves as humans and are successful because they are wired to want to be different and stop at nothing to be a game-changer. They don't completely give up their ethnic identity; they just don't see being Asian as any hindrance to achieving their goals.

Many Asian Americans struggle with the desire to be loved by the people around them. That desire isn't a problem until they become overly absorbed in their self-image, needing to be perceived as successful or cool. Hiro, on the other hand, emphasized that you must tune out noise from other people. When he was in college, a lot of students would graduate and go off to work in fields like banking or consulting. It's tough for me to not get jealous of others going into prestigious jobs, even if they are jobs that don't interest me — hence why I continued to do everything in my power to become an investment banker for so long.

Those prestigious jobs didn't appeal to Hiro, though, because he was putting his head down and working on Supplies for Dreams, which he thought added more value to society. He was also very confident that he wanted to do something that would help people, which meant he wanted to work at a company that actually built things people used. Hiro realized that consulting and banking companies don't exactly create products or services that most people utilize. Also, as a natural leader, he enjoyed the times when he could drive people toward a common goal and solve problems.

Because of these values, he ended up working at GE. He was very proud of the fact that he was working at a company making a lot of products foundational to many countries, including the biggest countries in the world like the United States and China. Beyond household appliances, GE makes jet engines and generators that help power industry in the world, and Hiro was proud that his company was adding so much value to the world.

He also wanted to work at a big company like GE because he wanted to get a lot of experience. He had been interested in entrepreneurship but didn't know if he had enough knowledge to actually start something meaningful. At GE he was able to understand how scaling businesses work and how to work in and lead groups.

Hiro understood his values and thus was able to find purpose and happiness in his work. This is extremely tough if you don't understand what your values are in the first place. Constantly gaining more understanding of yourself will help you to find your purpose and passion in life.

What can Rebels learn from Hiro?

Tune out the noise. Stop caring about what others think.

It's an almost innate desire to chase prestige. This urge is further amplified by stereotypes that expect Asians to be in professions that are seen as most prestigious.

If you ask most people, they would say they would not want to work for a job solely because of its prestige. But why is it so hard to decide between taking a more prestigious job and one less so? It's because they're lying to themselves. We care too much about our self-image. We want to belong and want people to think that we are awesome. Guess what? Most people don't care where you work or how much money you make. We're selfish beings who care more about ourselves. Hiro was special in that he was able to tune out noise from others and really pursue what he wanted.

Learn what your strengths and weaknesses.

I always hated the interview question, "What are your biggest strengths?" The question I hated even more was, "What are you biggest weaknesses?" Why? Because I didn't fully know the answer myself. It felt as though knowing myself more would expose my flaws further; it was too easy to self-criticize in a non-constructive manner.

I've made an effort to better understand these strengths and weaknesses, and while hard at first, I have seen myself grow. Knowing your strengths doesn't mean you fall back on them in every situation and ignore improving your weaknesses. However, it also doesn't mean never taking advantage of your strengths. Hiro was special in that he understood that he possessed leadership abilities, whether that was innate or learned. Because of that strength, he chose a career that would challenge him in that particular area and allow him to develop his skills.

Confidence. Confidence. Confidence.

Perhaps the underlying reason why people are so self-critical and focused on their image is that they lack confidence. It is a stereotype that Asians are more passive and less assertive. Humility is often a core value in Asian culture, but humility does not necessarily cause a lack of confidence.

I firmly believe confidence is skill that can be improved, which means you can practice being more confident. That often involves going out of your comfort zone and finding things that you normally wouldn't pursue. Often times, that means meeting new people who can help you.

* * *

Li Jiang was one of the people who helped me see that there was so much more out there in life to pursue, changing my mindset regarding life and career. I first met Li as a sophomore at an Entrepreneurship Summit held at Northwestern. I asked him how he got into his current job as a venture capitalist and instead of answering me directly he asked me what I wanted to do in life. At that time, I was still incredibly conflicted because my goal was to be an investment banker, but that desire was not quite so strong anymore, so when I told him I wanted to be a banker I felt like a fraud. I don't remember what exactly he said, but it seemed like he could see through me. A year later, I reached out again to Li to talk with him about his upbringing and how he got to the place he is today.

Li Jiang is the chief evangelist at GSV Asset Management, as well as an angel investor who has helped set up summits that have featured speakers like former President Barack Obama. He started the largest student-run startup at Northwestern as a freshman in 2006. To top that off, he created a popular

YouTube documentary on the Silicon Valley. Crazy.

Li was born in Chengdu, China, but his parents moved to Canada and then the United States for graduate school when he was young, and eventually his family settled in a nice North Atlanta suburb when he was nine. The area was surprisingly diverse and was around 30 to 40% Asian.

His parents wanted him to do well, and they may have fit a lot of Asian parent stereotypes, but as a kid Li was very much independent. He did debate in high school, which helped him get better at speaking and perhaps become more Americanized. Li describes his younger self as rebellious, and although it's hard to pinpoint why, he says his grandmother — who was very outspoken, aggressive and ambitious — may have played a role, since he lived with her and his grandfather from age three to nine.

He also told me that back in Georgia, he used to put chairs on parking spots and sell them for money. Clearly, his entrepreneurial spirit was already shining through. Li eventually came to Northwestern for undergrad. His parents wanted him to go to Northwestern, but he strongly considered Michigan State and Miami of Ohio—again a testament to his desire to be different and act rebellious.

In college he had the idealistic vision of being like Bill Gates and dropping out to start a company. By a stroke of luck, he met a friend in the first week of school who was interested in starting a company. They started Campus Solutions and learned an incredible amount from the experience. **He believed that "you can only learn so much in the classroom" and still holds this view today.**

This view isn't revolutionary: I've heard people often say that in their summer internships or first year at a job they learned more than all their years of college combined, but that doesn't revolutionize how people view school. Li's view is that you can learn so much outside the classroom, not just during the summer or after college, but during your time at college as well. For me this idea is hard because I valued my grades so much in high school. My freshman year was a shock to me because for the first time I felt like I was being challenged in my classes. I was sleeping at 3 a.m., studying for hours, and still not doing as well as I wanted. It was straight A's in high school, and in college…it was not.

Li, however, had a different mindset from a lot of students in college. He claims he "didn't really respect school," meaning although he knew grades were important, he didn't let an A, B, or C define him and his self-worth. What he found more interesting were projects outside of the classroom, like his startup. Along with growing it to become the largest student-run company at Northwestern, he learned the soft skills of how to manage people and work with others in a real-world situation — something he couldn't have learned directly from school.

It's hard to wrap your mind around this concept if you've held your worth in grades for so long. Yes, good grades are nice. But there are always ways to market yourself to companies beyond grades. It's starting projects outside the classroom that allows you to distinguish yourself. There are, of course, some exceptions. Unfortunately, if your goal truly in your heart is to become doctor, good grades are important to get into a good medical school. If you want to attend graduate school, grades are once again an integral part. But beyond that, grades are less important than you think, despite what your parents say or what you believe.

Earlier in college, I often looked at my LinkedIn and resume and thought to myself that I was a bad candidate for any job. I had some experience, but no name brands except my school, and even that wasn't as solid a name brand as Harvard, Princeton, or MIT. It took me a while, but I eventually realized that while companies love to see name brands, it also helps a lot to be interesting. I realized then that my resume was not interesting. I was doing what everybody else was doing and perhaps not to as high a degree. That made me think: How could I make myself more interesting? How could I stand out now that I wasn't the top student like I was in high school? I realized that of the successful and awesome people I saw on

LinkedIn, many of them started projects outside of school that nobody tells you to do. They had ideas and just sought out to do them. These are the types of projects Li is talking about.

And it's not just starting a company in college that he believes in. He told me that you can do any project that interests you: starting a club, creating a community of people on social media that have similar interests as you, writing a blog...the list goes on.

So why not start that learning by pursuing passion projects while still in school? Li emphasizes the fact that starting some type of project in college might be the best possible time to start because it is almost risk-free. That's how he viewed starting a startup in his first week of freshman year. He didn't have to worry about getting an internship for the summer his freshman year nor worry about supporting a family. Also, because he was at college, he could leverage resources from the school and professors. Most importantly, he was surrounded by a ton of students from diverse backgrounds who could aid him with his ambitions.

Even if you're not in school Li believes you should go for your project ideas. As Carl Jung, the famous psychiatrist, said, "You are what you do, not what you'll say you do."

Li doesn't believe grades are unimportant... They are. But,

he is saying that you have more free time than you think to pursue projects. Examine all the times when you aren't being productive. Are you spending it with friends? That's good; maintaining a social life is critical. Are you spending time with Netflix? That's also good, because it helps maintain your sanity. But then question how much time you spend hanging out with people, watching movies/shows, and using social media — it's probably too much. There is always time in the day to do something extra. The most successful people are those who make the most of their days by pursuing those passion projects, while others think about them but never start them.

There are so many projects you can pursue. Write a blog, create a podcast, make YouTube videos, or become a social media star. Maybe you really like chess and coding. Why not try to build an AI chess bot that can beat you? Maybe you are really into politics. Why not remotely help someone on their campaign? Maybe you like marketing. Why not interview successful marketers and write a blog?

Other people have also realized that side projects are important. Georgetown adjunct professor Eric Koester "studied 3,400 of the most successful young people under the age of 30 — each of the Forbes 30 Under 30 alumni since 2011. What Eric realized is that more than 85% of these individuals created something — a book, a podcast, a video series, a conference

or something similar. And that act of creation helped demonstrate expertise and create credibility in hyper-powerful ways."

CHAPTER 8

BRUCE LEE OF HAIRCUTTING – THE TRAILBLAZERS

———

As the self-proclaimed "Bruce Lee of Haircutting," Ray Fung sees haircutting radically differently than others do, which has led him to start an International Hair Design Institute and author multiple books on hair design.

Ray Fung was born in Hong Kong to a mother from Shanghai and a father from Guangzhou (Canton). As the youngest of six kids, he didn't get as much individual attention from his parents as other kids do. While he grew up in a housing project in Hong Kong, he never felt poor. His parents didn't have that much money and Ray says that "they knew who they were" because they understood their place in society. Because of how he was raised, Ray claims he grew up with fewer expectations from his parents; since he didn't grow up with much, the only place he felt he could go was up.

As an adult, he started his own hair salon in 1993. After a couple years in the industry, however, he realized people weren't thinking about haircutting correctly. Instead of just doing the same haircut over and over, Ray made sure everyone's hair was unique and treated it as "design" rather than "styling" or "cutting." He started doing drawings of every hair design he gave. What drove him was his desire to learn and research more about hair design. He felt that hairdressing was an overlooked industry. Everyone gets a haircut, but there hasn't been much innovation in the space. His goal was and still is to change the thinking that haircutting is just something we do every so often. He eventually had over a thousand drawings and decided to share his findings with the world in the multiple books he published. He firmly believes that he is changing the world.

When I asked him how his cultural identity affected his work, he explained that he doesn't think about it in his work. If you are good, he says, then people will pass over your skin tone. Of course, he believes, "Deep down you better be good," because nobody will you give you credit for being mediocre.

Ray then told me a story about John Lennon. When Lennon was younger, in elementary school, his teachers asked him what he wanted to be when he grew up. All the other kids were saying, "firefighter, astronaut, inventor, doctor." But instead Lennon responded, "I just want to be happy." Ray believes that's a human condition: that we should strive to be happy. If you want to find passion in life, do what makes you happy. The point is that finding passion in life doesn't have to be tied to racial identity. He doesn't treat himself as an Asian who happens to live in America. "Nobody is white," he says. Because if you are in the United States, your identity is also tied to being American, where everybody comes from a different background. **We all, as Americans, have a common understanding that we can have the freedom and the ability to move up in life while finding happiness and success.** That is what we all should value much more than being part of a certain race that burdens us in the United States.

* * *

For Kaitlyn Yang, neither race, gender, nor physical appearance deterred her from reaching her goals.

Kaitlyn was born in Zhengzhou, China, with limited motor abilities. When she was younger, she was still able to walk, but at school, her grandmother would wait for the bell to help Kaitlyn go up and down the stairs between classes because schools in China were relatively inaccessible for the disabled. Her parents soon realized it wasn't a viable long-term solution for Kaitlyn and her grandmother, so they wanted to move. Kaitlyn's father applied for a research grant at Washington University in St. Louis and was accepted, so the family immigrated to America when she was nine.

Quickly after arriving, she was diagnosed correctly with spinal muscular dystrophy and started using a wheelchair at school. For Kaitlyn, moving to America meant leaving family and friends. In China, everyone knew about her disability and accepted her; it felt normal for her there, but moving to another country meant starting over. She felt like a "sore thumb" for being in a wheelchair in the United States and remembers getting a lot of stares from other kids.

Even though she was enrolled in an ESL program, her parents searched for another easy and affordable way to teach her English. Their solution was to give her a Blockbuster card so she could watch movies with English subtitles; they also got her a computer so she could learn to type in English.

She would watch a movie after school every day and soon became pretty good at English. Whenever she got Blockbuster DVDs, she always watched the second disk that had all the behind-the-scenes footage; for her, these second disks were sometimes better than the actual movie. She vividly remembers watching a second disk for one of the Star Wars movies that went through the job of each person involved in the movie, from makeup to visual effects all the way up to director. When she saw the visual effects role, she realized it might be something she would want to do in the future. As she grew older and the internet became more prevalent, she began researching online everything she could find out about visual effects and checked out all the books she could find on the subject from the library.

Meanwhile, her parents wanted her to focus on academics. Both her mother and father did research at Washington University at St. Louis and had degrees in medicine from China. Her parents were strict: For example, they expected her to maintain a 4.0 GPA. They were not, however, helicopter parents always making sure she was studying. She understood her parents' expectations and took them as a given. Kaitlyn maintained that 4.0 GPA, but that didn't prevent her from pursuing her interest in art.

She took a lot of art classes in middle school and high school. Eventually, she took a graphics design class and knew immediately it was the type of art that she wanted to pursue. Afterward, she started making a portfolio to apply for film school.

When it was time for her to apply to college, her parents wanted her to go to Wash U and study medicine. Because

Kaitlyn didn't want to be a doctor, the compromise with her parents was for her to get into Wash U and study something else. However, in the back of her mind she knew she wanted to do VFX and wouldn't get the best opportunity to do that at Wash U. In fact, she actually hoped to not get into Wash U. Perhaps fate, of the seven colleges she applied to, the only one she was rejected from was Wash U! She was accepted into USC's film school, the top film school in the world.

Since she didn't get into Wash U she made two other compromises with her parents: Instead of studying medicine, she would at least do computer science. Also, since she was going to move to LA, they agreed that she would have to pay for all living expenses. So, Kaitlyn went to USC and took a couple CS classes in addition to her animation studies.

Kaitlyn knew she had to work to afford rent, food, and textbooks, so she began working in film as soon as she started at USC. As time went on, she worked on bigger and bigger freelance gigs. She freelanced for the U.S. Army and was the main editor for the HowTo channel on YouTube. By the end of college, she already had basically four years of experience in film.

Eventually, she found her way to working at the best VFX company in the world in 2013. It had been her dream to work there. However, after a month or two, she became disillusioned by the bureaucracy. Aware that it was mostly white men in the field, she went off to start her own VFX studio at the suggestion of her friend. Her success as the VFX supervisor and co-founder of Alpha Studios landed her a spot on the Forbes 30 Under 30 list.

Just as there was discrimination in the industry, Kaitlyn also explained to me how it has always been a fight with her parents in terms of her career path. But, over the years, they have eased up. When at dinner with her parents as a kid she remembers their enthusiasm when talking about the research or work they were doing. As she described, "It became their everyday talking point." Similarly, her parents have seen how VFX has been the "talking point" and passion for Kaitlyn over the past 10 years. That's what made them more lenient and understanding of her.

Looking back, she understands her parents' thought process. Being a doctor or lawyer is a tried and true path. Once you get a medical or law degree, your life is pretty much set. Her parents wanted her to take a path that was risk-free and stable. Kaitlyn told me, "Part of the luxury for our generation [1.5 or 2nd generation immigrants]: Our folks have taken a less risky route, so we have the chance to take those risks."

Her biggest takeaway she wanted to leave with me? Now more than ever, you don't have to work for one company forever and have the more traditional career. In fact, you can work for yourself. It also doesn't have to be last resort: It can be first resort!

CHAPTER 9

FROM AWKWARD KID TO RAPPER - THE IGNORED

———

A self-proclaimed normal American kid who grew up liking Pokémon and Power Rangers, Awkwafina is anything but normal now. She broke out as a rapper with her hit music video for "My Vaj" in 2012 and now she's an actress in *Ocean's 8* and *Crazy Rich Asians*, the first movie since *Joy Luck Club* in 1993 to feature a predominantly Asian cast. Although she didn't fit the mold of what an Asian "should act and look like," she was able to tune out the noise and pursue her dreams.

Born Nora Lum, she grew up in a single-parent home because her mother passed away when she was four. Awkwafina said that as a kid, she was not incredibly good at anything. Her father wanted her to play piano or violin, but she didn't want to play music until she discovered trumpet herself when she was 11. She believes that she got pretty good at it because nobody forced her to practice. Because of her love for trumpet, she attended the music and performing arts school LaGuardia High where most people there were quite exceptional at music and practiced a lot.

Always be learning and improving yourself.

While Awkwafina realized she was not the best student, that didn't mean she was apathetic toward learning, academic or not. She was constantly curious and found many of her idols in music form online.[1]

Her father didn't respect her relationship with music, however. If you weren't a prodigy, then you weren't good. If you didn't get A's, then you weren't smart. There was no middle ground for him. In her mind, though, she knew she didn't want to do something that she didn't fully want. She went after her interests instead and pursued digital music in college.

After college, she had made some music and filmed a video for her song "My Vaj." Her boss at the time told her not to post the video because people would see it and she'd never get hired again. Awkwafina had come to a crossroads: She wasn't content with her current job and didn't want to work in an office feeling unhappy forever. She saw her friends happy with their lives, but she wasn't. She was taking a risk by posting the video — but another part of her mind wondered what would happen if the video brought her fame. Perhaps because she had less to lose than someone who had been caught up in pursuing a prestigious job all their life, she took the risk and posted the video.

Her father at first was adamantly against her career as a rapper, but one day at work her dad saw her on the cover of New York Magazine and instantly called her to congratulate her.

Take risks to be happy instead of doing what makes your parents happy.

Similar to my advice for the Good Kids, parents will come around to whatever you do eventually if you are successful. Rap was something Awkwafina did for herself and without the risks she took to publish that music video she wouldn't have found that success.

* * *

Steve Ly is the mayor of Elk Grove, California. In fact, he made history because he became the first Hmong American mayor ever in 2016. "It is significant for the Hmong community, but more importantly this is an American story," Ly said. "It doesn't matter whether you came to America 20 years ago or

200 years ago, everyone has a story, and when you reach into the story of every individual in the United States you see the meaning of what America is about."[2] Ly humbly understands that everyone in the United States has a different background and that many people who have come from other countries have found success in America. He added, "Obviously, you can't deny the fact that I am an ethnic minority; you can't deny the fact that I came to this country at four years old as a refugee." But he has embraced this fact, saying, "That's exactly what makes America great, the fact that our country continues to be a beacon of freedom for immigrants and refugees who come from all over the world to make something of themselves."

Despite the "model minority" and other negative stereotypes, Asian Americans who have been ignored are finding success in many different ways. We continue to romanticize the idea of the "American Dream" in which everyone that comes to the United States is given fair treatment and equal opportunity. Of course, that's not actually how things play out in reality. At the same time, complete cynicism precludes any sort of progress. We need to be hopeful for the future that things will improve — and if we are hopeful, we will have a better mindset when it comes to working, studying and ultimately pursuing our dreams.

There are millions of Americans who share similar stories of success. They come from poor families or are refugees, but they find a way to work hard and succeed in America. In their stories, we can find inspiration, motivation and hope.

CHAPTER 10

YOUTUBER STARS AND ICE SKATING QUEENS – THE NEW MAJORITY

Do you remember watching KevJumba, Nigahiga, Wong Fu, Happy Slip, Timothy DeLaGhetto, David Choi, Kina Grannis, and Fung Bros? These Asian Americans took advantage of a media platform that democratized video-sharing. YouTube allowed anybody with a camera, computer, and internet connection to share whatever they wanted. These were my role models growing up: people who were Asian American like me. They made jokes about their strict parents and having the pressure to get A's in school. Finally, there were famous people I could relate to who understood my upbringing.

Many of these early YouTubers still make videos. Wong Fu Productions in particular focuses on creating videos with Asian American culture as the central theme. The YouTube channel started with Phil Wang making videos his junior year of high school. He continued to make videos in college at UCSD where he met Ted Fu and Wesley Chan in a school production. Together they created videos for Wong Fu, but none of them considered film as a serious career.

At first unconsciously, Wong Fu's films consistently featured Asian Americans including Wang, Fu, and Chan themselves. "I didn't have a very diverse group of friends," Wang explained. "I was an Asian kid with a lot of Asian friends growing up in California and in the UC system...[but] over the years, it's become more conscious, our choices of representation have a larger ripple effect."[1]

Wong Fu's recent film series "Yappie" is about Andrew, an Asian American in California who works as a software developer. More and more, he realizes that growing up Asian has shaped who he has become. He realizes he's just like all the other Asians he knows — Asians content to live in a bubble, while pursuing safe, comfortable jobs as opposed to getting out of the comfort zone.

A caption on Phil Wong's Instagram reads, "A turning point in the development of #Yappie happened last year when I hit a roadblock and someone asked me 'Who is Andrew?' I thought for a bit and realized, Andrew is me if Wong Fu never happened. Maybe not an engineer (not smart enough) but def at a 9-5 thinking/wishing I could do something more. If that's you, don't worry, you didn't make the wrong choice, don't quit your job or change your major tomorrow…but think about what really brings you joy, think about how you can make a difference in the world. Little by little, give into it, indulge in it, work at it. You might be surprised where it'll take you."[2] As Phil points out, it's not necessary to make radical changes to your life, but the first step is to notice where you can make improvements. That might be going to a yoga class for the first time to get in shape or going on stage to perform slam poetry in front of people you don't know to practice public speaking. At first, it's tough to get out of your shell, but only practice will make you better.

A reason I particularly like Wong Fu films is because they *appreciate the work of all ethnic groups.* "[Asian Americans] don't have one common struggle, one common mission. 'Crazy Rich Asians' — not my narrative, but it's going to enable another movie. 'Master of None' — not my narrative, but it empowered me to make my version," Phil said. "I hope someone sees 'Yappie' and says, 'That's cool, but I'm going to tell my southern Vietnamese story growing up around all Hispanic people,' or whatever your story is."[1] Phil hopes to empower all Asian Americans, not just the ones like him and there's something to learn from this goal. If we appreciate not only our own culture, but that of others, Asian or not, we can really begin to see racial barriers being torn down.

It's important to also explore your identity.

Wong Fu did so by addressing different Asian American themes in their videos, whether in "Yellow Fever," where they discuss Asian woman dating white guys, while it's hard for Asian guys to date white girls, or "Yappie," in which they discuss Asian professional life. Understanding your relationship to being Asian is important. Do we accept the stereotypes placed upon us? Are we limiting ourselves because we believe that the world limits us? These are important questions to think about and come to terms with.

Wong Fu is a role model for the New Majority because their videos highlight and analyze Asian American culture—something deeply personal to themselves and desperately lacking in film. Through humorous, yet honest portrayals of Asian American life today, Wong Fu has created a large, buzzing internet community to connect all Asian Americans alike.

* * *

Mirai Nagasu became the first U.S. woman ever to land a triple axel in an Olympics at the 2018 games in PyeongChang. In a triple axel, skaters take off facing forward and spin three and a half rotations in the air. It's so hard that only two other women in history have ever landed the jump at the Olympics. Like with most famous athletes, we usually only see the glory moments and ignore the work and failures along the way.

When Mirai was 16, she placed fourth overall at the 2010 Vancouver Olympics. However, she missed the 2014 Olympics when three other skaters were chosen instead, despite placing third at the 2014 U.S. Championships. Having experienced so much success when she was young, only to see her dream of medaling at the Olympics slip away in 2014, was devastating.

Mirai's confidence was shaken. "There are moments when I think I'm not very smart and not very pretty, and skating is the only thing that stands out about me," she said. "It's like the love of my life. When you love someone, sometimes you want to break up."

We're different from our parents. But we should always thank them and give credit where it's due.

Despite all the challenges, she continued to push through, and she credits a lot of her work ethic to her parents. Her family owns a sushi restaurant in the LA suburb Arcadia, and she remembers watching her parents work long hours there. "I used to sleep there," she recalled. "I used to basically live there." Her father often refused to take vacations because he felt obligated to work and be able to pay his employees. Mirai translated her parents' work ethic at the restaurant to her ice skating. Like a lot of successful Asian Americans, she is thankful for her parents' support. They were so influential in her life that the she couldn't have gotten to the point she's at without them.[3]

It seems also that her parents were not just hard workers, but also incredibly humble. A regular customer who remembers seeing Mirai doing homework at the restaurant once said, "Her parents told us, 'She ice-skates,' but ... we never knew until we saw a clipping of her winning the nationals. Then we said, 'She really ice-skates.'" Mirai is definitely grateful and proud of her parents for their influence in her life.

It's inevitable that more stars like Mirai will emerge in the coming years as the New Majority grows. Let's not forget that behind the spotlight of sports fame is a close-knit, humble family that values hard work. Mirai captures the essence of sticking to her roots by emulating her parents humbleness and hard work. That is and will continue to be important for the New Majority.

CONCLUSION

———

There once was a kid who grew up in the suburbs of Cleveland, Ohio. He grew up playing outside with his older sister and neighbors, watching *Tom and Jerry* on TV and reading *Magic Tree House*. He remembers listening to Avril Lavigne on his sister's Walkman and later Coldplay on the first-generation iPod Nano. He ate fish sticks and pretzels for snacks on weekends and took road trips with his family throughout the United States. Later, he played saxophone in band and sang in choir. In high school, he was a swimmer for four years on the varsity team.

There was also another boy who lived in the same town. He attended Chinese school on Saturdays and Sunday School at the Chinese Church. Tuesdays were for piano lessons. Monday through Friday he did math problems out of workbooks. For dinner his mother prepared egg and tomato, as well as ground beef and lettuce stir-fry. He watched "Monkey King" on VCD. He flew to China in the summers to visit grandparents, aunts, uncles, and cousins because the only family members he had in the United States were his mom, dad, and sister. In high school, he practiced SAT problems after school and got straight A's in class.

If you didn't guess: Both those kids are me. This is my story — my story as an Asian American growing up. It shaped who I am today and the goals I have for life. It's allowed me to have a diverse experience in life, but also it created conflicts in my mind: "My life is so different from all my white friends; I wish I had a normal life like them" or "Nobody understands me fully. If only I could just share with people what my life is like and have them understand me."

My hope is that by bringing to light at least some stories of Asian Americans you will have a better understanding that you are not alone. There are people like you who have shared similar struggles. We keep our thoughts and feelings bottled up because we feel different from the majority of America, but we should make our voices heard. Even if we all have different upbringings, experience, and values, as Asian Americans we can sympathize with the similarities we share. As part Asian, we all should appreciate our culture and our parents who grew up very different from us. As part American, we should hold dearly onto the values of freedom and non-judgement of all shapes, sizes, and colors.

Furthermore, your story is unfinished. Planning for your future is beneficial, but the path you envision in never as smooth as you hope. That shouldn't discourage you, because the beauty of life is the twists and turns you encounter. Keep big picture goals in mind, but be flexible and open to what truly brings you happiness and enjoyment in life. The five different paths in this book are just a guide, and I've given you examples of how successful Asian Americans have followed these paths. It's up to you, however, to fill out the details.

My call to action for you is to ask yourself how being Asian American has affected your life choices up to this point. After reflection, if you're unhappy with how you have been living your life then I want you to make *one* change to your life after reading this book. It only has to be one. If you do, I guarantee you'll have greater peace with what you want to do in life. You will doubt your choices less and pursue what you want more. Instead of feeling weighed down by race, you will feel the freedom and purpose to break through and reach those higher goals.

I am very hopeful for all Asian Americans out there and the generations to come. So, let us set out on our path and find that success desired not by our parents and not by our society, but by ourselves. I look forward to hearing your stories.

ACKNOWLEDGEMENTS

———

First, I'd like to thank Eric Koester, professor of entrepreneurship at Georgetown University. Thank you for reaching out to me in the first place and for eventually convincing me to write this book. It was a huge learning experience, and I loved your enthusiasm for me and my work from the start till the end.

In addition, I'd like to thank Head of Publishing at New Degree Press, Brian Bies for patiently supporting me throughout the whole process. Your help along with the editors, layout designers, and other members of New Degree Press made this book a reality.

To all the people I interviewed—I appreciate that you took time out of your day to talk with me. Your stories are the backbone of this book, and I hope that people will be inspired by your journeys and experiences.

Thanks to all my early readers—the feedback and support was invaluable. Also, to my friends who probably thought I was crazy when I told them I was writing a book: Thanks for not doubting me and for always being curious about my progress.

Mom and Dad, I appreciate you for providing for me and for sending me to college. Thank you for shaping me into who I am today and for instilling in me pride for my culture and heritage. I'm also grateful to my sister for fielding tons of questions from me and for bragging about me to her friends. I'm thankful always for your love and encouragement.

A final thanks to my readers: You are already part of a bigger movement to change this world we live in and redefine what people think it looks like to be an American today. You are all my inspiration. Thank you.

APPENDIX

INTRODUCTION

Bradsher, Sam Borden and Keith. "Tight-Knit Family Shares Lin's Achievement." *The New York Times*, The New York Times, 25 Feb. 2012, www.nytimes.com/2012/02/26/sports/basketball/tight-knit-family-shares-lins-achievement.html.

López, Gustavo, et al. "Key Facts about Asian Americans, a Diverse and Growing Population." Pew Research Center, Pew Research Center, 8 Sept. 2017, www.pewresearch.org/fact-tank/2017/09/08/key-facts-about-asian-americans/.

Editor, The Muse. "Everything You Need to Know About Jeremy Lin." *Free Career Advice*, The Muse, 12 Feb. 2012, www.themuse.com/advice/everything-you-need-to-know-about-jeremy-lin.

Editor, The Muse. "Everything You Need to Know About Jeremy Lin." *Free Career Advice*, The Muse, 12 Feb. 2012, www.themuse. com/advice/everything-you-need-to-know-about-jeremy-lin.

"15 Million People Were Self-Employed in 2015, or 10.1 Percent of All U.S. Workers." *U.S. Bureau of Labor Statistics*, U.S. Bureau of Labor Statistics, 1 Mar. 2016, www.bls.gov/spotlight/2016/ self-employment-in-the-united-states/home.htm.

Peck, Buck GeeDenise. "Asian Americans Are the Least Likely Group in the U.S. to Be Promoted to Management." *Harvard Business Review*, 31 May 2018, hbr.org/2018/05/ asian-americans-are-the-least-likely-group-in-the-u-s-to-be-promoted-to-management?utm_campaign=digest&utm_medium=email&utm_source=nuzzel.

Peck, Buck GeeDenise. "Asian Americans Are the Least Likely Group in the U.S. to Be Promoted to Management." *Harvard Business Review*, 31 May 2018, hbr.org/2018/05/ asian-americans-are-the-least-likely-group-in-the-u-s-to-be-promoted-to-management?utm_campaign=digest&utm_medium=email&utm_source=nuzzel.

Torres, Monica. "Research: Asian Americans Least Likely to Be Promoted to Management in Tech." *Ladders | Business News & Career Advice*, Ladders | Business News & Career Advice, 26 June

2018, www.theladders.com/career-advice/research-asian-amer-
icans-the-least-likely-to-be-promoted-to-management-in-tech.

Simms, Margaret. "'Model Minority' Myth Hides the Economic
Realities of Many Asian Americans." *Urban Institute*, 8 June 2017,
www.urban.org/urban-wire/model-minority-myth-hides-eco-
nomic-realities-many-asian-americans.

Chen, Liyan. "How Asian Americans Can Break Through The Bamboo Ceiling." *Forbes*, Forbes Magazine, 20 Jan. 2016, www.forbes.
com/sites/liyanchen/2016/01/20/how-asian-americans-can-
break-through-the-bamboo-ceiling/.

Wingfield, Adia Harvey. "The Professional Burdens of Being a 'Model
Minority." *The Atlantic*, Atlantic Media Company, 6 June 2016,
www.theatlantic.com/business/archive/2016/06/profession-
al-burdens-model-minority-asian-americans/485492/.

HOW TO USE THIS BOOK

Sealy, Ruth, and Val Singh. "The Importance of Role Models in the
Development of Leaders' Professional Identities." *Leadership
Perspectives*, 2008, pp. 208–222., doi:10.1057/9780230584068_15.

CHAPTER 1

Lee, Jennifer. "We Need More Asian American Kids Growing up to

Be Artists, Not Doctors." *The Guardian*, Guardian News and
Media, 16 Mar. 2014,

CHAPTER 3

"John Cho of 'Selfie': 'I Experienced Racism.'" *The Washington Post*,
WP Company, 9 Oct. 2014, www.washingtonpost.com/news/
morning-mix/wp/2014/10/09/john-cho-of-selfie-wants-roles-
outside-any-asian-stereotype-2/?utm_term=.5c509462c3b8.

Chin, Christina B, et al. *TOKENS ON THE SMALL SCREEN: Asian
Americans and Pacific Islanders in Prime Time and Streaming
Television.* AAPI's on TV, 2017, pp. 1–13, *TOKENS ON THE
SMALL SCREEN: Asian Americans and Pacific Islanders in
Prime Time and Streaming Television.*

"Inequality Remains about the Same in Hollywood Films, USC
Study Finds." *USC News*, 22 Feb. 2018, news.usc.edu/106914/
inequality-remains-about-the-same-in-hollywood-films-new-
usc-study-finds/.

Levin, Sam. "'We're the Geeks, the Prostitutes': Asian American
Actors on Hollywood's Barriers." *The Guardian*, Guardian News
and Media, 11 Apr. 2017, www.theguardian.com/world/2017/
apr/11/asian-american-actors-whitewashing-hollywood.

"John Cho On Acting And 'Columbus.'" *NPR*, NPR, 4 Aug. 2017, www.npr.org/2017/08/04/541538785/john-cho-on-acting-and-columbus.

Chung, Nicole. "John Cho in 'Columbus' Is John Cho as You've Never Seen Him Before." *GQ*, GQ, 4 Aug. 2017, www.gq.com/story/john-cho-columbus-interview.

CHAPTER 4

Kandil, Caitlin Yoshiko. "After 50 Years of 'Asian American,' Advocates Say the Term Is 'More Essential than Ever.'" *NBCNews.com*, NBCUniversal News Group, 31 May 2018, www.nbcnews.com/news/asian-america/after-50-years-asian-american-advocates-say-term-more-essential-n875601

Wagner, Alex. "America's Unseen Minority." *The Atlantic*, Atlantic Media Company, 13 Sept. 2016, www.theatlantic.com/politics/archive/2016/09/why-dont-asians-count/498893/.

Yam, Kimberly. "Asian-Americans Have Highest Poverty Rate In NYC, But Stereotypes Make The Issue Invisible." *The Huffington Post*, TheHuffingtonPost.com, 8 May 2017, www.huffingtonpost.com/entry/asian-american-poverty-nyc_us_58ff7f40e4b0c-46f0782a5b6.

"U.S. Poverty Statistics." *Federal Safety Net*, 2017, federalsafetynet.com/us-poverty-statistics.html.

Kochhar, Rakesh, and Anthony Cilluffo. "Key Findings on the Rise in Income Inequality within America's Racial and Ethnic Groups." *Pew Research Center*, Pew Research Center, 12 July 2018, www.pewresearch.org/fact-tank/2018/07/12/key-findings-on-the-rise-in-income-inequality-within-americas-racial-and-ethnic-groups/.

Espenshade, Thomas J., et al. "Admission Preferences for Minority Students, Athletes, and Legacies at Elite Universities*." *Social Science Quarterly*, vol. 85, no. 5, 2004, pp. 1422–1446., doi:10.1111/j.0038-4941.2004.00284.x.

Kim, Caitlin. "Why Asian Americans Don't Vote." *New America*, 7 Sept. 2017, www.newamerica.org/weekly/edition-175/why-asian-americans-dont-vote/.

CHAPTER 5

Blevins, Jason. "Chloe Kim Becomes Youngest to Win X Games Gold, Unseats Kelly Clark." *The Denver Post*, The Denver Post, 26 Apr. 2016, www.denverpost.com/2015/01/24/chloe-kim-becomes-youngest-to-win-x-games-gold-unseats-kelly-clark/.

"Teen Chloe Kim Takes X Games Gold." *U.S. Ski & Snowboard*, 25 Jan. 2015, usskiandsnowboard.org/news/teen-chloe-kim-takes-x-games-gold.

Yean, Ricky. "Asian-Americans Are Cultural Orphans (Aka I Hope Crazy Rich Asians Isn't a Flop)." *Medium*, Augmenting Humanity, 9 July 2018, medium.com/@rickyyean/asian-americans-are-cultural-orphans-aka-i-hope-crazy-rich-asians-isnt-a-flop-fo1eccof9b1.

"U.S. Census Bureau QuickFacts." *U.S. Census Bureau*, www.census.gov/quickfacts/fact/table/US/PST045217.

Chowkwanyun, Merlin, and Jordan Segall. "The Rise of the Majority-Asian Suburb." *CityLab*, 27 Aug. 2012, www.citylab.com/equity/2012/08/rise-majority-asian-suburb/3044/.

"Asian Students at UCLA, UCSD and UC Berkeley: The Price of Success?" *The College Solution*, 10 Jan. 2011, www.thecollegesolution.com/asian-students-at-ucla-ucsd-and-uc-berkeley-the-price-of-success/.

Thompson, Derek. "Everybody's in a Bubble, and That's a Problem." *The Atlantic*, Atlantic Media Company, 27 Jan. 2017, www.theatlantic.com/business/archive/2017/01/america-bubbles/514385/.

CHAPTER 6

Chua, Amy. *Battle Hymn of the Tiger Mother*. Bloomsbury Publishing, 2014.

CHAPTER 9

TEDxTalks. "The Life and Times of an Underachiever | Nora 'Awk-wafina' Lum | TEDxStuyvesantHS." *YouTube*, YouTube, 16 Dec. 2014, www.youtube.com/watch?v=Smnbr5wNMyY.

Wang, Frances Kai-Hwa. "For Nation's First Hmong Mayor, Life Is an 'American Story.'" *NBCNews.com*, NBCUniversal News Group, 13 Dec. 2016, www.nbcnews.com/news/asian-america/nations-expected-first-hmong-mayor-life-american-story-n695341.

CHAPTER 10

Lee, Traci G. "After a Decade on YouTube, Wong Fu Productions Still Has a Story to Tell." *NBCNews.com*, NBCUniversal News Group, 19 June 2018, www.nbcnews.com/news/asian-america/after-decade-youtube-wong-fu-productions-still-has-story-tell-n881606

Wang. Selfie. *Instagram*, 2 Apr. 2017. www.instagram.com/p/BlugcsNn-c1/?taken-by=wongfuphil.

Ford, Bonnie D. "A Star Reborn -- Figure Skater Mirai Nagasu Reclaims Her Olympic Story." *ESPN*, ESPN Internet Ventures, 20 Feb. 2018, www.espn.com/espnw/culture/feature/article/22451122/a-star-reborn-figure-skater-mirai-nagasu-reclaims-olympic-story.

www.ingramcontent.com/pod-product-compliance
Lightning Source LLC
Chambersburg PA
CBHW071524180526
45171CB00002B/367